中国〔海南〕南海博物馆

海上丝绸之路系列展览 之

海上丝绸之路上的峇峇娘惹文化展

EXPLORING THE WORLD OF BABA NYONYA
A PERANAKAN CULTURE EXHIBITION ON THE MARITIME SILK ROAD

中国（海南）南海博物馆 编

CHINA (HAINAN) MUSEUM OF THE SOUTH CHINA SEA

科学出版社

北 京

图书在版编目（CIP）数据

峇峇娘惹的世界 : 海上丝绸之路上的峇峇娘惹文化展 / 中国（海南）南海博物馆编. --北京 : 科学出版社, 2025.3. -- ISBN 978-7-03-079896-1

Ⅰ. K883.002

中国国家版本馆CIP数据核字第20244V5R01号

责任编辑：张亚娜　周　娲

责任校对：张亚丹

责任印制：张　伟

书籍设计：北京美光设计制版有限公司

峇峇娘惹的世界——海上丝绸之路上的峇峇娘惹文化展

中国（海南）南海博物馆　编

科学出版社 出版

北京东黄城根北街16号

邮政编码：100717

http://www.sciencep.com

北京汇瑞嘉合文化发展有限公司印刷

科学出版社发行　各地新华书店经销

*

2025 年 3 月第　一　版　开本：787×1092　1/8

2025 年 3 月第一次印刷　印张：33 1/2　插页：7

字数：490 000

定价：308.00 元

（如有印装质量问题，我社负责调换）

主办单位

中国文物保护基金会
中国（海南）南海博物馆

支持单位

亚洲文化遗产保护基金
晶致非梵（天津）文化科技发展有限公司

鸣谢单位

腾讯公益慈善基金会
信德集团有限公司
泰康保险集团股份有限公司
中国银行股份有限公司
贵州茅台公益基金会

展览组织与实施

总策划	辛礼学　赵　晶
总统筹	朱　磊
策展人	李其仁
内容策划	李其仁　彭　文
形式设计	何其潮　潘乐茵　赵雪君　陈淑玲 吴伟义
文物点交	辛礼学　李其仁　陈子晗
文物布展	郑睿瑜　李其仁　吴伟义　符晓遥 林佩珊　苟新文汝　赵珏琪　陈子晗 谢丽萍　等

图录编委会

主编	辛礼学
副主编	朱　磊
执行主编	李其仁
英文翻译	亓　浩　等

致辞

　　海上丝绸之路是东西方交通往来和经济贸易之路，也是一条文化交流之路、文明互鉴之路。东南亚地区作为海上丝绸之路途经的重要区域，早在15世纪，一些福建或广东潮汕等地区的华人便已移民至此。在这里，他们与当地社区融合相处，通婚生子，形成了一个新的融合遗产社区，被称为"峇峇娘惹"。历经数代人的奋斗，他们为东南亚地区的社会发展作出了重要贡献，也将中华文化与在地文化相融，形成了独具特色的"峇峇娘惹"文化。

　　中国（海南）南海博物馆按照中央有关指示精神，紧扣"一带一路"倡议，精准定位，重点做好文物研究展览、国际交流合作、水下文物保护等方面工作，积极打造"21世纪海上丝绸之路"文化交流的重要平台。2024年3月—7月，我馆与中国文物保护基金会共同举办"峇峇娘惹的世界——海上丝绸之路上的峇峇娘惹文化展"。此次展览通过展出新加坡文博机构124件（套）文物及我馆馆藏土生华人家具，以文物和史料为依托，兼顾通俗性与专业性，多角度展示峇峇娘惹文化内涵及特点。该展览作为我馆"海上丝绸之路"系列展览的又一延续，既是展示我馆与海上丝绸之路沿线国家和地区文化交流方面的优秀成果，又体现了中华文化与世界文化间的相互包容与共同发展。

　　中国与新加坡一衣带水，两地人文交流历久弥新。我馆将以此次展览为契机，用展览架起彼此间友谊的桥梁，开展文明间的交流和对话，加深双方文化交流互鉴，为中新文化交流与发展贡献力量。

　　最后，感谢所有为这次展览付出辛勤努力的工作人员，也希望这本图书能够成为更多人了解峇峇娘惹文化、海上丝绸之路历史的重要媒介。

中国（海南）南海博物馆馆长

Greetings

The Maritime Silk Road serves as a vital conduit for transportation, economic trade, cultural exchange, and mutual learning between Eastern and Western civilizations. Southeast Asia, a crucial region along this route, has been a destination for Chinese immigrants, particularly from Fujian and Chaoshan region of Guangdong, since as early as the 15th century. These immigrants integrated with local communities, intermarried, and formed a new hybrid heritage community known as the "Baba Nyonya". Over the generations, they have made significant contributions to Southeast Asia's social development, while blending Chinese and local cultures to create the distinctive "Baba Nyonya" culture.

The China (Hainan) Museum of the South China Sea, in accordance with central government directives, closely aligns with the "Belt and Road" initiative. The museum has positioned itself accurately, focusing on cultural relics research and exhibition, international exchange and cooperation, and underwater cultural heritage protection. It actively strives to establish itself as a significant platform for cultural exchanges along the "21st Century Maritime Silk Road". From March to July 2024, our museum collaborated with the China Cultural Heritage Foundation to present the exhibition "Exploring the World of Baba Nyonya: A Peranakan Culture Exhibition on the Maritime Silk Road". This exhibition showcased 124 artefacts from Singaporean cultural institutions alongside our museum's collection of Peranakan Chinese furniture. Based on cultural artefacts and historical materials, the exhibition maintained a balance between academic depth and public accessibility, presenting the essence and characteristics of Baba Nyonya culture from multiple perspectives. As a continuation of our museum's Maritime Silk Road exhibition series, this exhibition not only highlighted the fruitful outcomes of cultural exchanges between our museum and countries along the Maritime Silk Road but also exemplified the mutual inclusiveness and shared development between Chinese culture and world cultures.

China and Singapore are closely connected by sea, with a rich foundation of cultural exchange between the two regions. The China (Hainan) Museum of the South China Sea will seize this exhibition as an opportunity to build a bridge of friendship between them, fostering exchanges and dialogues between civilizations, deepening mutual cultural understanding, and contributing to the cultural exchange and development between China and Singapore.

Finally, we extend our gratitude to all staff members who have dedicated their efforts to this exhibition. We hope that this catalogue will serve as a significant medium for more people to gain insights into Baba Nyonya culture and the history of the Maritime Silk Road.

Xin Lixue

Director, China (Hainan) Museum
of the South China Sea

致辞

　　东南亚是多元土生社群的家园，其共同特征在于文化的融合：将各自的祖先文化，包括华人、印度人、阿拉伯人、欧洲人等不同背景，融入到马来群岛的本土文化之中。新加坡土生文化馆以展示这些社群为荣，他们不仅包括被称为"峇峇娘惹"的土生华人，还包括土生印度人（或称马六甲的仄迪人）、爪哇土生人，以及土生阿拉伯人。

　　本次展览呈现的是土生华人社区的文化。在其历史进程中，峇峇娘惹既传承了先辈的中华文化，又与所定居的东南亚社群密切交流，吸收同化，形成了一派充满活力的多元融合文化。这既体现在他们的物质文化上，也反映在非物质文化遗产中。独特的语言、美食、衣着、社交习俗和艺术形式，都是上述交流的产物。

　　如今，新加坡、马来西亚和印度尼西亚掀起了复苏土生文化的浪潮，土生手工艺品、时装、美食日益流行。尽管这些习俗和传统随着数世纪的时代变迁而有所演变，许多土生人群依然对其多元包容的文化遗产怀有深深的认同感，并由衷地引以为傲。土生社群让我们意识到秉持多元开放社会的宝贵价值。

　　本次展览所展示的东南亚土生华人文化，是中国（海南）南海博物馆、新加坡亚洲文明博物馆和土生文化馆团队多年努力的成果。我衷心感谢中国（海南）南海博物馆的密切合作，感谢该馆辛馆长及其团队对土生文化的兴趣和相关展览策划；感谢新加坡亚洲文明博物馆和土生文化馆的策展和收藏团队，以及新加坡国家文物局文物保护中心的收藏和保护团队，他们不辞辛劳，将借展文物从新加坡运至中国，使其得以顺利展出；最后，还要感谢代表中国（海南）南海博物馆组织本次展览的晶致非梵（天津）文化科技发展有限公司。

　　展览内容告诉我们，无论站在历史的角度，还是置身于当下视野，文化交流都让我们的生活更加多姿多彩。我们希望此次的展览与合作不仅让中国观众了解峇峇娘惹的文化，还能激发他们的浓厚兴趣，吸引其前往新加坡土生文化馆，进一步了解更多土生社群和相关文化。

新加坡亚洲文明博物馆馆长
新加坡土生文化馆馆长

Greetings

Southeast Asia is home to diverse Peranakan communities whose unifying trait is the blending of ancestral cultures — Chinese, Indian, Arab, European, and others — with the indigenous cultures of the Malay Archipelago. The Peranakan Museum is proud to showcase these communities, which comprise not only the Chinese Peranakans, also known as the "Baba Nyonya", but also the Peranakan Indian or Chitty Melakans, the Jawi Peranakans, and the Arab Peranakans.

This exhibition features the culture of the Chinese Peranakan community. In the course of their history, the Baba Nyonya have inherited the Chinese culture of their forefathers and have also closely interacted and assimilated with the Southeast Asian communities they settled in, forming a vibrant hybrid culture that can be seen in both their material culture as well as their intangible cultural heritage. Distinctive languages, cuisines, ways of dress, social customs and artistic forms arose from these interactions.

Aspects of Peranakan culture are now the focus of revival across Singapore, Malaysia, and Indonesia. Peranakan crafts, fashion, and cuisine are increasingly popular. While these customs and practices may have changed over the centuries, a keen sense of identity and pride in the diversity and inclusiveness of their multicultural heritage remains among many Peranakans. The Peranakan communities remind us of the value of diverse and open societies.

This exhibition showcasing the Chinese Peranakan culture of Southeast Asia is the culmination of several years of work by the teams at the China (Hainan) Museum of the South China Sea, and the Asian Civilisations Museum and Peranakan Museum. I would like to warmly thank the China (Hainan) Museum of the South China Sea for its close collaboration on this exhibition. We thank Director Xin and his team at the China (Hainan) Museum of the South China Sea for their interest in looking at Peranakan culture, and for their curation of this exhibition. I would also like to recognise the curatorial and collections teams at the Asian Civilisations Museum and Peranakan Museum, as well as the collections and conservations teams at the National Heritage Board's Heritage Conservation Centre who worked tirelessly to bring the loan artefacts from our collection from Singapore to China so that they could be featured in the exhibition. Finally, thanks to Jingzhi Feifan (Tianjin) Culture and Technology Development Co., Ltd, who acted on behalf of the China (Hainan) Museum of the South China Sea in organising this exhibition.

The content of this exhibition reminds us all that cultural exchanges enrich all our lives, whether when viewed from a historical lens, or from the contemporary perspective. We hope that this collaboration, and this exhibition, will enable visitors not only to learn of the culture of the Baba Nyonya, but also build further interest and encourage more Chinese visitors to the Peranakan Museum to learn about the other Peranakan communities and cultures.

Clement Onn

Director, Asian Civilisations Museum and
the Peranakan Museum

目录
Contents

引言 Preface

　　东南亚地区是海上丝绸之路途经的重要区域，早在15世纪，一些福建或广东潮汕等地区的华人移民到东南亚。在这里，他们与当地社区融合相处，通婚生子，形成了一个新的融合遗产社区，被称为"峇峇娘惹"。历经数代人的奋斗，他们为东南亚地区的社会发展作出了重要贡献，也将中华文化与当地文化相融，形成了独具特色的"峇峇娘惹"文化。

　　Southeast Asia was an important region along the Maritime Silk Road. As early as the 15th century, Chinese immigrants from regions like Fujian and Chaoshan region of Guangdong started migrating to Southeast Asia. Over time, these immigrants integrated, married, and had children with localcommunities, forming a new mixed heritage community known as "Baba Nyonya". Through several generations of hard work, they have made significant contributions to the social development of Southeast Asia. Meanwhile, they have also integrated Chinese culture with local cultures, creating the unique "Baba Nyonya" culture.

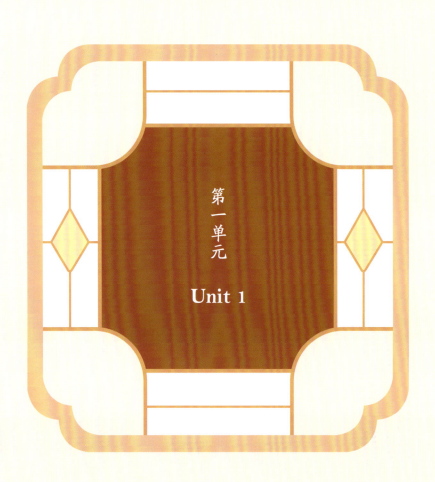

第一单元

Unit 1

创造历史的一代先驱

峇峇娘惹的先辈们秉承着中国人民的进取精神，跨洋过海来到了东南亚，成为历史的开拓者和一个新社区的先驱者。他们成功地将丰富的中华文化传统与定居的东南亚社群的生活方式相融合，不仅为后代开辟了一个新天地，更为当地社会经济发展作出了突出贡献。

The Pioneers of History Creation

The ancestors of Baba Nyonya, inheriting the undaunted spirit of the Chinese people, crossed the ocean and arrived in Southeast Asia to become the pioneers of history and a new community. They successfully infused the rich tapestry of Chinese cultural traditions with the way of life of the Southeast Asian communities they settled in. This synthesis not only forged a fresh horizon for their descendants but also significantly propelled the socio-economic advancements within their new locale.

『峇峇娘惹』社区的形成

　　明代，随着中国航海技术的发展和海上丝绸之路的不断拓展，居住在东南沿海地区的人们航行到东南亚，与当地各国进行商贸往来，其中的一部分人最终定居在印尼和马来半岛，与当地社群通婚，融入了当地的生活，形成了最早的"峇峇娘惹"。这些"峇峇娘惹"与之后"下南洋"的华人有所不同，他们在当地居民中拥有较高的社会地位。

　　东南亚拥有多元的Peranakan或土生文化社群，峇峇娘惹社区是其中之一。峇峇（Baba）娘惹（Nyonya），或称为土生华人（Peranakan Chinese），是15世纪初定居在东南亚一带的中国移民和当地原住民所生的后代。Peranakan这个词来源于马来语词根anak，意思是孩子。"峇峇娘惹"的名称出现于明清时期，男子被称为"峇峇"，主要负责对外参加社会事务；女子被称为"娘惹"，主要管理家中事务。

东南亚地区的早期
中国移民

据《汉书·地理志》记载："自日南障塞、徐闻、合浦船行可五月，有都元国……黄支之南，有已程不国，汉之译使自此还矣。"说明最晚在两汉时期，中国的海商就已前往东南亚各地与之进行海上贸易，且来回路程均需通过马六甲海峡。

唐代，东南亚诸国已有华人移民。但移民数量较少，还未能形成社群。

宋元之后，中国移民逐渐增多。15世纪初，东南亚地区出现中国移民聚居区。郑和下西洋前，爪哇的苏拉巴亚和苏门答腊的旧港，各有数千人聚居的中国移民社群。

Early Chinese Immigration in Southeast Asia

According to the "Geographical Records" in the *Han Shu* (Book of Han), it is documented, "From Rinan, Xuwen, Hepu, a journey by ship takes about five months, reaching the Duyuan Kingdom…south of Huangzhi lies the Kingdom of Yichengbu. Translators of the Han Dynasty returned from here." This indicates that, at the latest during the Han Dynasty, Chinese maritime merchants were already engaged in trade with various regions in Southeast Asia, and their round trips necessitated passing through the Strait of Malacca.

During the Tang Dynasty, there were already Chinese immigrants in various Southeast Asian countries. However, the number of immigrants was relatively small, and they had not yet formed distinct ethnic groups.

After the Song and Yuan Dynasties, the number of Chinese immigrants gradually increased. In the early 15th century, Chinese immigrant settlements began to emerge in Southeast Asia. Before Zheng He's voyages to the West, there were Chinese immigrant communities with several thousand residents in Surabaya, Java, and the old port of Sumatra.

The Formation of the "Baba Nyonya" Community

During the Ming Dynasty, advancements in Chinese maritime technology led residents from China's southeastern coastal regions to navigate towards Southeast Asia, engaging in commerce with local countries. Some of these settlers eventually established themselves in Indonesia and the Malay Peninsula, formed unions with local Southeast Asian peoples, weaving their lives into the fabric of the local communities, and giving rise to the earliest "Baba Nyonya" communities. These "Baba Nyonyas", different from later immigrants to "the South Seas", held a relatively high social status among local residents.

Southeast Asia is home to diverse Peranakan or native cultural communities; the Baba Nyonya community is one of them. "Baba" and "Nyonya" also known as Chinese Peranakans or Straits Chinese, are the descendants of Chinese immigrants who settled in Southeast Asia in the early 15th century and intermarried with the local indigenous people. The term "Peranakan" originates from the Malay root word "anak" which means child. The term "Baba Nyonya" emerged during the Ming and Qing dynasties. Men were referred to as "Baba", mainly responsible for engaging in external social affairs, while women were called "Nyonya", primarily managing household affairs.

（一）明清时期的移民

Immigration During the Ming and Qing Dynasties

大规模的东南亚华人社区的形成始于明朝，盛于清朝。16世纪初期，土生华人社群开始出现在印尼和马来半岛。到19世纪，土生华人社区的人们已经在槟城、马六甲、新加坡和雅加达站稳脚跟。新加坡作为英国在海峡殖民地的首府，同时也是一个繁荣的港口，吸引着来自各个地区的土生华人。此外，在缅甸、泰国、印尼其他地区等，也有成熟的土生华人社群，并且如今依然存在。

The substantial formation of the Southeast Asian Chinese community began during the Ming Dynasty and peaked during the Qing Dynasty. Chinese Peranakan communities began developing in Indonesia and the Malay Peninsula in the early 16th century. By the 19th century, Peranakans were well established in Penang, Malacca, Singapore, and Jakarta. Singapore, the capital of the British colony of the Straits Settlements and a thriving port, attracted Peranakans from across the region. Additionally, there were established Peranakan communities across wider Southeast Asia such as Myanmar, Thailand, and other parts of Indonesia, which are still present today.

（二）"峇峇娘惹"社区的最终形成

The Final Formation of the "Baba Nyonya" Community

随着华人移民的不断增多，他们与当地土著的通婚也不断增加，最终形成了语言文化上融合，发展为"峇峇娘惹"社区，即东南亚的土生华人社群。

土生华人的文化根源是中华文化，但在其发展过程中受到了东南亚本土文化和欧洲文化的影响。因此，无论是语言、宗教信仰、文化习俗，还是身份认同，都有其自身的独特文化。独树一帜的峇峇娘惹社区的形成，体现了中华文化和接纳了中国移民的东南亚文化的包容与创新。

With the continuous increase of Chinese immigrants, the frequency of their intermarriages with the local indigenous peoples also grew, eventually leading to a blend of languages and cultures, marking the emergence of the "Baba Nyonya" community, also known as the Peranakan Chinese communities of Southeast Asia.

Although the cultural roots of the local-born Chinese people lie in Chinese culture, their development process was influenced by the local culture of Southeast Asia and European culture. Hence, their language, religious beliefs, cultural traditions, and identity recognition have all formed a unique culture of their own. The formation of the distinctive Peranakan community is a testament to the inclusiveness and innovation of both the Chinese culture and the cultures of Southeast Asia that received these immigrants from China.

陈明远夫妇肖像画

约19世纪90年代

纵91厘米，横69厘米

新加坡亚洲文明博物馆 藏

Tan Choon Hoe夫妇 赠

Portraits of Mr and Mrs Tan Beng Wan

Around 1890s

Height 91 cm, width 69 cm

Asian Civilisations Museum, Singapore

Gift of Mr and Mrs Tan Choon Hoe

这两幅肖像画描绘的是一对土生华人，陈明远（Tan Beng Wan）夫妇。陈明远先生出生于越南，被新加坡土生华人船主陈金殿收养。他们的服饰融合了东南亚和中国元素，是土生华人文化的标志。肖像画中陈明远先生身着中国传统服装，这是当时土生华人男性的标准搭配，直到20世纪初他们才开始穿着西式服装。

陈明远夫人身着长衫，胸前以三枚胸针固定，长衫罩着里面的裙布，是那时东南亚女性的常规穿着。她旁边放着一套槟榔用具及一个瓷痰盂。直到20世纪中期，嚼槟榔的习惯仍在东南亚地区广泛流行。

These two portraits depict a Peranakan Chinese couple, Mr and Mrs Tan Beng Wan. Mr Tan Beng Wan was born in Vietnam and adopted by Tan Kim Tian, a prominent Peranakan Chinese ship owner in Singapore. Their dress is a mix of Southeast Asian and Chinese elements that are a hallmark of Chinese Peranakan culture. In the portraits, Mr Tan Beng Wan is attired in traditional Chinese clothing, which was the standard attire for Peranakan Chinese men at that time. It wasn't until the early 20th century that they began adopting Western-style clothing.

Mrs Tan Beng Wan is portrayed wearing a long gown with three brooches securing the front, over a skirtcloth. This was a common outfit for Southeast Asian women of the time. She is accompanied by a betel set and a porcelain spittoon. The practice of chewing betel nut remained widely prevalent in Southeast Asia until the mid-20th century.

黑檀嵌螺钿扶手椅

19世纪末至20世纪初
新加坡亚洲文明博物馆 藏

Heitan Inlaid Mother-of-Pearl Armchair
Late 19th to early 20th century
Asian Civilisations Museum, Singapore

黑檀嵌螺钿扶手椅

19世纪末至20世纪初

新加坡亚洲文明博物馆 藏

Heitan Inlaid Mother-of-Pearl Armchair

Late 19th to early 20th century

Asian Civilisations Museum, Singapore

19世纪末至20世纪初

新加坡亚洲文明博物馆 藏

Heitan Inlaid Mother-of-Pearl Square Table
Late 19th to early 20th century
Asian Civilisations Museum, Singapore

　　早期的土生华人偏爱镶螺钿的黑檀家具。在传统的土生华人家庭中，嵌螺钿家具几乎一直算是家庭正式会客厅的一部分，多用于招待客人以及婚礼和葬礼等特殊场合。

　　In the early days, Peranakans favored *Heitan* furniture adorned with mother-of-pearl inlay. Within the traditional Peranakan households, furniture embellished with mother-of-pearl was nearly always part of the formal receiving hall of the traditional Peranakan home, which was used for hosting guests and special occasions such as weddings and funerals.

粉彩开光凤穿牡丹纹痰盂

19世纪末至20世纪初

高37.1厘米，口径35.2厘米

新加坡亚洲文明博物馆 藏

Tony Wee 和 Colin Holland 遗赠

Famille-Rose Phoenix Amidst Peony Spittoon

Late 19th to early 20th century

Height 37.1 cm, mouth diameter 35.2 cm

Asian Civilisations Museum, Singapore

Bequest of Tony Wee and Colin Holland

槟榔盒套装

19世纪
盒长25厘米，宽15厘米，高22.5厘米
新加坡亚洲文明博物馆 藏

Betel Nut Set
19th century
Length 25 cm, width 15 cm, height 22.5 cm
Asian Civilisations Museum, Singapore

　　嚼槟榔在土生家庭中非常流行，同时也是招待客人的习俗。槟榔套装通常包含槟榔叶、槟榔果和石灰等。可选的配料包括棕儿茶、丁香和烟草，咀嚼出的红色汁液吐在陶瓷痰盂中。一套基本的槟榔盒套装包括槟榔切割器和盛食材的容器。

Chewing betel nut was highly popular in Peranakan households, serving as one of the customary treats offered to guests. The betel nut ensemble typically included betel leaves, areca nuts, and slaked lime. Optional ingredients consisted of gambier, cloves, and tobacco. The red-hued saliva generated from chewing was expelled into a ceramic spittoon. A fundamental betel nut set comprised a betel nut cutter and containers for holding the ingredients.

峇峇话

由于与当地居民通婚,"峇峇娘惹"社区发展出了一类自己的混合语言,即峇峇话。峇峇话大体上可以分为两类,峇峇马来话和峇峇福建话。峇峇马来话主要是马六甲峇峇的语言,后因许多人搬迁到新加坡而传播过去。在印尼的雅加达,峇峇马来话也称为"华人马来话(*Melayu Tionghoa*)",语言的混合情况十分类似。而峇峇福建话则主要在槟城使用。

峇峇马来话与标准马来语有三个明显的差别:一是词汇,峇峇马来话混杂了许多汉语和英语的舶来词汇;二是语音,峇峇马来话的许多词汇发音与标准马来语不尽相同;三是语法,峇峇马来话的语法多受汉语影响,跟标准马来语有异。

比如在人称代词方面就有明显区别,峇峇话大都根据福建话而称呼"我""你"为 gua、lu,不用马来语 aku、engkau。可是,针对第三人称或复词,如"他"和"我们",峇峇话就说马来语的 dia 和 kita。

对于亲属的称呼,峇峇话向来是遵循华人习惯,长幼有序。

峇峇式马来语是早期"峇峇娘惹"身份认同的独特象征。虽然许多年轻的土生华人已不再讲,但是他们仍在推广语言课程、土生戏剧(*wayang Peranakan*)和诗歌(*pantun*)等,努力复兴这门语言。

峇峇福建话主要是指槟城的峇峇方言,它以闽方言为主,夹杂着马来语和英语中的舶来词汇。因此有学者认为峇峇福建话更像是汉语方言,而不像峇峇马来语那么混杂。

Baba Malay

Due to intermarriage with local residents, the "Baba Nyonya" community developed its distinctive mixed language known as the Baba language. Baba language can be broadly categorized into two types: Baba Malay and Baba Hokkien. Baba Malay is primarily the language of the Babas in Malacca, later brought to Singapore as many people relocated there. In Jakarta, Indonesia, Baba Malay is also known as "Chinese Malay" (Melayu Tionghoa) showing a linguistic similarity in the mixing of languages. Baba Hokkien is concentrated in Penang.

Baba Malay differs from Standard Malay in three distinct aspects: vocabulary, pronunciation, and grammar. In terms of vocabulary, Baba Malay incorporates many Chinese and English loan words. Pronunciation in Baba Malay differs from that of Standard Malay. Additionally, the grammar of Baba Malay is often influenced by Chinese, making it distinct from Standard Malay.

For example, there are noticeable differences in pronouns. Babas commonly use the Hokkien terms "gua" and "lu" for "I" and "you" respectively, instead of the Malay terms "aku" and "engkau". However, when referring to third parties or plurals such as "he", "they" and "we" Babas use the Malay terms "dia" and "kita".

In terms of addressing relatives, Baba Malay follows Chinese customs with specific terms for particular relatives based on order of family hierarchy.

Baba style Malay is a unique symbol of identity for the "Baba Nyonya". While many younger Chinese Peranakans no longer speak the language, there are efforts to revive it through the promotion of language lessons, Peranakan theatre (wayang Peranakan), and poetry (pantun).

Baba Hokkien refers to the Baba dialect of Penang. It is mainly based on Hokkien, with loan words from Malay and English, Therefore, some scholars argue that Baba Hokkien is more akin to a Chinese dialect rather than being as mixed as Baba Malay.

19

二
先驱者的非凡人生

作为跨越传统的先驱们，土生华人在政治、经济、教育、卫生、宗教、文化等领域颇有成就，他们身兼多职，成为本地商业和政坛的开路先锋；他们人脉通达，网络遍布东南亚甚至更远的区域，为海上丝绸之路的繁荣作出了贡献。

19世纪，土生华人已在一些重要领域担任领导者，并顺理成章地成为当时华人社群的领袖，他们为华人争取着更多的权利。

Extraordinary Lives of the Trailblazers

As pioneers who transcended traditions, the Peranakan Chinese achieved significant accomplishments in fields such as politics, economics, education, healthcare, religion, and culture. They held multiple positions, becoming pathfinders in local business and governing fields; and they were well-connected. They had extensive networks across Southeast Asia and beyond. By the 19th century, the Peranakan Chinese began to serve as leaders in some important fields, naturally becoming the leaders

（一）1819—1889年：商务与社区的发展

1819—1889: Business and Community Development

1819年，英国在新加坡设立港口，其后陆续有中国人移居此地。当时一些最富有且最具权势的华商是土生华人。其中，热衷慈善事业的家族往往担任社群领导。

In 1819, when the British set up a port in Singapore, Chinese gradually arrived. Some of the wealthiest and most influential Chinese businessmen at the time were Peranakan Chinese Among them, families that were passionate about charity often served as community leaders.

陈笃生

Tan Tock Seng

1798—1850

福建社区早期杰出领袖
Prominent Early Leader of the Fujian Community

陈笃生，祖籍漳州海澄，生于马六甲。他的家族早年来到马六甲，他随后前往新加坡寻求商机。后来，他通过经营土产生意积累了财富，并与英商怀特黑德（J. H. Whitehead）合伙经营，遂成巨富。

作为新加坡福建社区的领袖，陈笃生带头成立天福宫，此处后成为福建社区的聚集点。他是新加坡第一位受封为太平绅士的亚洲人。陈笃生还创建了一家帮助穷苦华侨的医院，他的慈善事业至今仍被世人所称颂。

Tan Tock Seng was born in Malacca to a family originally from Haicheng, Zhangzhou. His family had relocated to Malacca in earlier years and he later moved to Singapore to look for business opportunities. Later, he accumulated wealth through running the business of local specialties, and formed a partnership with the English merchant J. H. Whitehead, becoming immensely prosperous.

As a leader within the Fujian community in Singapore, Tan Tock Seng took the initiative to establish Thian Hock Keng Temple, which later became a focal point for the Fujian community. He was the first Asian to be conferred the title of Justice of the Peace in Singapore. Tan Tock Seng also founded a hospital to aid impoverished Chinese immigrants, earning enduring praise for his philanthropic works.

陈若锦

Tan Jiak Kim

1859—1917

著名土生华人
Reknowned Peranakan Chinese

陈若锦是陈金声之孙、陈明水之子。他加入金声公司，并在海峡殖民地立法议会以及其他政府组织任职。1900年，他与林文庆、宋旺相共同创办了英籍海峡华人协会。陈若锦还大力支持教育，捐款建设新加坡女子学校，协助开办医学院。1915年，达尔比希尔（C. W. Darbishire）评论像陈若锦这样的领导人"胸襟足够开阔，能够接纳西方思想，并将东、西两方观点融会贯通"。

Tan Jiak Kim was the grandson of Tan Kim Seng and the son of Tan Beng Swee. He joined Kim Seng & Company and served in various capacities in the Straits Settlements Legislative Council and other governmental organizations. In 1900, he founded the Straits Chinese British Association along with Lim Boon Keng and Song Ong Siang. Tan Jiak Kim ardently supported education, generously contributing to the establishment of the Singapore Chinese Girls' School and assisting in the founding of a medical college. In 1915, C. W. Darbishire noted that leaders like Tan "are broadminded enough to grasp the Western point of view and to weld it easily and smoothly with the Eastern point of view".

黄
仲
涵
（1866-1924）
像

1887年

纵16.6厘米，横10.9厘米

新加坡土生文化馆 藏

Lee Kip Lee夫妇 赠

Oei Tiong Ham (1866-1924)

1887

Height 16.6 cm, width 10.9 cm

Peranakan Museum, Singapore

Gift of Mr and Mrs Lee Kip Lee

黄仲涵是来自爪哇三宝垄的土生华商和社区领袖。他的公司从事多种贸易活动，包括19世纪90年代的鸦片贸易。到1900年，他的公司成为荷属东印度群岛主要的蔗糖生产商，后来又成为亚洲最大的华资公司。1896年，荷兰殖民地政府任命他为三宝垄华人社区的代表，负责协助处理华侨事务。1920年，黄仲涵从三宝垄永久移居新加坡。

Oei Tiong Ham was a Peranakan Chinese businessman and community leader hailing from Semarang, Java. His company engaged in various trade activities, including trade related to opium in the 1890s. By 1900, his company was the leading sugar producer in the Dutch East Indies, and later became the largest Chinese-owned company in Asia. In 1896, the Dutch colonial government appointed him as the representative of the Chinese community in Semarang tasking him with assisting in handling overseas Chinese affairs. In 1920, Oei Tiong Ham permanently relocated to Singapore from Semarang.

1862—1865年

纵13.5厘米，横6厘米

新加坡土生文化馆 藏

Lee Kip Lee夫妇 赠

『一半华人一半马来人混血』

"½ Chinese ½ Malay"

1862—1865

Height 13.5 cm, width 6 cm

Peranakan Museum, Singapore

Gift of Mr and Mrs Lee Kip Lee

著名苏格兰摄影师约翰·汤姆森（John Thomson，1837—1921）于1862年在新加坡开始他了的摄影生涯，并于此成立了第一间个人工作室。在他拍摄的众多作品中，有一些身着土生服饰的女性摆着西式姿势，如照片所示。

The celebrated Scottish photographer John Thomson (1837—1921) began his career in 1862 in Singapore, where he set up his first studio. Among his many subjects were women in Peranakan dress, arranged in Western-style poses, as here.

两位土生印度娘惹的工作室肖像照

约19世纪70年代

纵6厘米，横13厘米

新加坡土生文化馆 藏

Lee Kip Lee夫妇 赠

Studio Portrait of Two Peranakan Indian Nyonyas

Around 1870s

Height 6 cm, width 13 cm

Peranakan Museum, Singapore

Gift of Mr and Mrs Lee Kip Lee

这张照片的背面印有"G. R. Lambert & Co."字样。G. R. Lambert & Co. 有限公司成立于1867年，是新加坡一家先锋欧洲摄影工作室。

"G. R. Lambert & Co." is stamped on the verso of this photograph. Established in 1867, G. R. Lambert & Co. was a leading European photography studio in Singapore.

（二）1890—1945年：土生华人与海峡殖民地政府的合作

1890—1945: Cooperation Between Peranakan Chinese and the Straits Settlements Government

这一时期，许多允许华人任职的重要无薪政府岗位（包括了立法议会、市议会以及华人咨询局的委员）都由一小群颇具影响力的土生华人轮流担任，他们有些也是英籍海峡华人协会的领导人。

During this period, many significant unpaid government roles open to the Chinese—including positions in the Legislative Assembly, the City Council, and as commissioners on the Chinese Advisory Board—were occupied by influential Peranakan Chinese. Additionally, some of these individuals also held leadership positions within the Straits Chinese British Association.

宋旺相

Song Ong Siang

1871—1941

海峡华人历史学家、新加坡首位华人爵士
Straits Chinese Historian and Singapore's First Chinese to Receive a Knighthood

宋旺相，海峡华人历史学家，新加坡首位华人爵士，致力于海峡华人社区的改革。1894年，宋旺相创办新加坡首家罗马化的马来文报刊《东方之星》（Bintang Timor），后于1923年出版了代表性的《新加坡华人百年史》。他与林文庆、陈若锦携手创办了英籍海峡华人协会，并发行《海峡华人杂志》。宋旺相曾担任海峡华人教会主席，也曾是海峡华人教堂（现为布连拾街长老会磐石堂）的长老。

Song Ong Siang, a dedicated historian within the Straits Chinese community, devoted himself to the reform of the Straits Chinese community. In 1894, Song Ong Siang founded the first romanised Malay-language newspaper *Bintang Timor* (Eastern Star) and later published the influential *One Hundred Years' History of the Chinese in Singapore* in 1923. He collaborated with Lim Boon Keng and Tan Jiak Kim to establish the Straits Chinese British Association and published *The Straits Chinese Magazine*. He served as president of the Chinese Christian Association and was also an elder of the Straits Chinese Church, now Prinsep Street Presbyterian Church.

约20世纪30年代

纵13厘米，横18.5厘米

新加坡土生文化馆 藏

Lee Kip Lee夫妇 赠

土生华人全家福工作室肖像照

Studio Portrait of a Peranakan Family

Around 1930s

Height 13 cm, width 18.5 cm

Peranakan Museum, Singapore

Gift of Mr and Mrs Lee Kip Lee

1926年

纵8厘米，横11.9厘米

新加坡土生文化馆 藏

Lee Kip Lee夫妇 赠

Studio Portrait of a Peranakan Family

1926

Height 8 cm, width 11.9 cm

Peranakan Museum, Singapore

Gift of Mr and Mrs Lee Kip Lee

20世纪早期

纵13.4厘米，横8.3厘米

新加坡土生文化馆 藏

Lee Kip Lee夫妇 赠

Studio-Portrait of a Peranakan Chinese Couple

Early 20th century

Height 13.4 cm, width 8.3 cm

Peranakan Museum, Singapore

Gift of Mr and Mrs Lee Kip Lee

去往博罗浮屠途中的
土生家庭旅行照

约20世纪30年代

纵8.4厘米，横10.8厘米

新加坡土生文化馆 藏

Lee Kip Lee夫妇 赠

Peranakan Family on a Trip to Borobodur

Around 1930s

Height 8.4 cm, width 10.8 cm

Peranakan Museum, Singapore

Gift of Mr and Mrs Lee Kip Lee

1935年

纵28.3厘米，横25.9厘米

照片由Krishnan Pillay提供

Chitty Melaka Wedding Couple M. T. Pillay and Papathy

1935

Height 28.3 cm, width 25.9 cm

Image courtesy of Krishnan Pillay

Muthukrishnan Tevanathan Pillay于1897年出生于马六甲，于20世纪30年代移居新加坡，在会计总署担任行政主管至1958年。由于在第二次世界大战期间作出的贡献，他被英王乔治六世授予员佐勋章。

Muthukrishnan Tevanathan Pillay was born in Malacca in 1897. He migrated to Singapore in the 1930s and worked as an executive in the Accountant General's Office until 1958. He was appointed an MBE by King George Ⅵ for his contributions during the Second World War.

20世纪

纵8.4厘米，横10.8厘米

照片由Ahmad bin Mohamed Ibrahim家人提供

Dr S. I. M. Ibrahim and Family

20th century

Height 8.4 cm, width 10.8 cm

Image courtesy of the family of Ahmad bin Mohamed Ibrahim

这张爪哇土生家庭照片拍摄于Mohamed Ibrahim bin Shaik Ismail博士位于新加坡武吉知马的家中。他站在最右边，他的妻子Hamidah坐在右起第三位。他的儿子Ahmad bin Mohamed Ibrahim坐在最左边，他后来成为新加坡第一任总检察长。他们家收养了一位名叫Rose的华人女孩，照片中站在Hamidah前面。

This Jawi Peranakan family photograph was taken at the home of Dr Mohamed Ibrahim bin Shaik Ismail in the Bukit Timah district of Singapore. He stands at the far right, his wife Hamidah is seated third from right. His son, Ahmad bin Mohamed Ibrahim, who went on to become Singapore's first Attorney-General, is at the far left. Their family adopted a Chinese girl named Rose, who stands in front of Hamidah.

约20世纪

纵13.3厘米，横18.5厘米

新加坡土生文化馆 藏

Lee Kip Lee夫妇 赠

身着新年服饰的华人儿童

Chinese Children in New Year's Dress

Around 20th century

Height 13.3 cm, width 18.5 cm

Peranakan Museum, Singapore

Gift of Mr and Mrs Lee Kip Lee

1925年

长25厘米，宽15厘米，高7厘米

新加坡土生文化馆 藏

Lim Kok Lian为纪念其祖父母Lim Boon Keng（林文庆）和Grace Pek Ha Yin而赠

Silver Engraved Cigarette Box

1925

Length 25 cm, width 15 cm, height 7 cm

Peranakan Museum, Singapore

Gift of Lim Kok Lian in memory of his grandparents Lim Boon Keng and Grace Pek Ha Yin

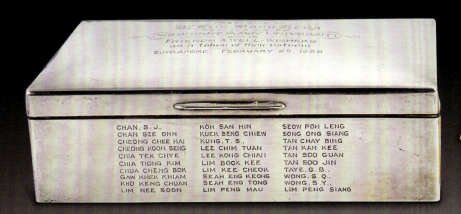

盒子上的铭文为"赠予厦门大学林文庆博士，他的朋友和祝福者以表敬意，新加坡，1926年2月25日"。这款纯银香烟盒由伦敦公司Henry Perkins & Sons于1925年制造。它于1926年由一群朋友和祝福者在新加坡赠送给林文庆博士。林文庆博士是20世纪早期著名的土生华人活动家，他是海峡殖民地和中国的教育改革倡导者，像许多东南亚土生华人一样，林博士与中国保持着文化和慈善上的联系。1921年，应陈嘉庚的邀请，林文庆成为中国厦门大学第二任校长，直至1937年。

The inscription on the box reads, "Presented to Dr Lim Boon Keng, President Amoy University, by his friends and well-wishers, as a token of their esteem, Singapore, February 25, 1926".

This silver cigarette box was manufactured by the London-based company Henry Perkins & Sons in 1925. In 1926, a group of friends and well-wishers in Singapore presented this box to Dr. Lim Boon Keng. Dr. Lim Boon Keng was a prominent early 20th-century Peranakan activist, advocate for education reform in the Straits Settlements and China. Like many Peranakans in Southeast Asia, Dr. Lim maintained cultural and philanthropic ties with China. In 1921, upon the invitation of Tan Kah Kee, Dr. Lim became the second president of Xiamen University in China, a position he held until 1937.

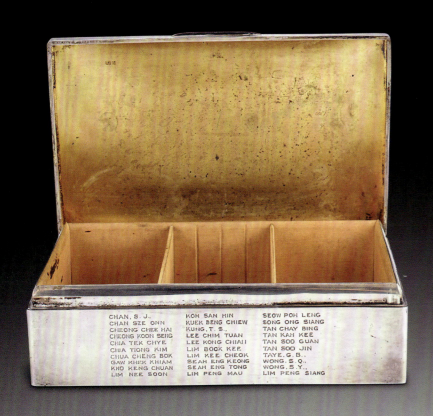

（三）1946—1965年：新加坡建国时期

1946—1965: The Founding Period of Singapore

第二次世界大战结束后，许多新加坡的新兴领袖皆来自受英文教育的土生华人社区。土生华人妇女也开始争取女性权益，为新加坡《妇女宪章》的制定作出了重要贡献，该宪章是促进性别平等的里程碑。

After World War II, many of Singapore's emergent leaders hailed from the Peranakan Chinese community, educated in English. Additionally, Peranakan Chinese women began to champion women's rights, significantly contributing to the establishment of Singapore Women's Charter, a landmark in the advancement of gender equality.

『马来歌谣』俱乐部

1955年
纵13.8厘米，横19.6厘米
新加坡土生文化馆 藏
Lee Kip Lee夫妇 赠

"Dondang Sayang" Club
1955
Height 13.8 cm, width 19.6 cm
Peranakan Museum, Singapore
Gift of Mr and Mrs Lee Kip Lee

第二单元

Unit 2

海上贸易推动的
文化融合

与东南亚地区的贸易往来，促生了峇峇娘惹社区的形成；其间，他们与不同文化群体进行的交流与合作，使得东南亚地区成为国际贸易的重要部分。这些反映了土生华人对社会发展作出的贡献，也充分展现了不同文明之间交流互鉴带来的成果。

Cultural Integration Propelled by Maritime Trade

Trade exchanges with the Southeast Asia region catalyzed the formation of the Baba Nyonya community. During this period, their interactions and collaborations with varied cultural groups played a pivotal role in establishing Southeast Asia as an essential component of international trade. Such dynamics underscore the significant societal contributions made by the Peranakan Chinese, while also highlighting the fruitful outcomes derived from the exchange and mutual learning among different civilizations.

土生饮食融合了中国、东南亚、南亚和中东饮食，并且受到了欧洲的影响。它是土生社区的重要生活传统之一，历经传承和演变，时至今日，我们能看到许多非常受欢迎的、经过地区甚至家庭改良过的土生美食。

Unique Peranakan Cuisine

Peranakan cooking fuses the cuisines from China, South Asia, and the Middle East with that of Southeast Asia, while also incorporating European influences. It is one of the community's key living traditions that continues to evolve today, and there are many regional and even family variations of well-loved dishes.

粉彩花鸟纹洗手碗

19世纪末至20世纪初

高8厘米，口径12.4厘米

新加坡亚洲文明博物馆 藏

Famille-Rose Finger Bowl with Flower and Bird Motifs

Late 19th to early 20th century

Height 8 cm, mouth diameter 12.4 cm

Asian Civilisations Museum, Singapore

1911—1930年

通高26厘米，口径18.4厘米

新加坡亚洲文明博物馆 藏

Tony Wee 和 Colin Holland 遗赠

Famille-Rose Kamcheng with Phoenix and Peony Motifs

1911—1930

Total height 26 cm, mouth diameter 18.4 cm

Asian Civilisations Museum, Singapore

Bequest of Tony Wee and Colin Holland

粉彩凤凰牡丹纹茶托盘

1911—1930年
长27.4厘米，宽20.9厘米，高2.4厘米
新加坡亚洲文明博物馆 藏
Tony Wee 和 Colin Holland 遗赠

Famille-Rose Tea Tray with Phoenix and Peony Motifs
1911—1930
Length 27.4 cm, width 20.9 cm, height 2.4 cm
Asian Civilisations Museum, Singapore
Bequest of Tony Wee and Colin Holland

粉彩牡丹纹酒杯

1911—1930年

高8厘米，口径9厘米

新加坡亚洲文明博物馆 藏

Tony Wee 和 Colin Holland 遗赠

Famille-Rose Wine Cup with Peony Motif

1911—1930

Height 8 cm, mouth diameter 9 cm

Asian Civilisations Museum, Singapore

Bequest of Tony Wee and Colin Holland

粉彩凤凰牡丹纹温酒器

1911—1930年

通高14厘米，口径10.5厘米

新加坡亚洲文明博物馆 藏

Tony Wee 和 Colin Holland 遗赠

Famille-Rose Wine Warmer with Phoenix and Peony Motifs

1911—1930

Total height 14 cm, mouth diameter 10.5 cm

Asian Civilisations Museum, Singapore

Bequest of Tony Wee and Colin Holland

土生华人厨房

The Chinese Peranakan Kitchen

厨房是土生华人家庭的核心地带。娘惹美食除了追求精细的准备和烹饪技巧，还对餐桌、餐具、进餐方式、布置摆设等十分讲究，呈现出别具一格的娘惹饮食文化。

The kitchen is the heart of the Chinese Peranakan household. Beyond its meticulous preparation and cooking methods, Nyonya cuisine places significant emphasis on the dining table setup, tableware, dining etiquette, and decor, all of which come together to define the unique Nyonya culinary culture.

粉彩凤凰牡丹纹盖盅

1911—1930年

通高17.5厘米，口径18厘米

新加坡亚洲文明博物馆 藏

Famille-Rose Chupu with Phoenix and Peony Motifs

1911—1930

Total height 17.5 cm, mouth diameter 18 cm

Asian Civilisations Museum, Singapore

粉彩凤凰牡丹纹茶壶

1911—1930年

高18厘米，底径13厘米

新加坡亚洲文明博物馆 藏

Tony Wee 和 Colin Holland 遗赠

Famille-Rose Teapot with Phoenix and Peony Motifs

1911—1930

Height 18 cm, bottom diameter 13 cm

Asian Civilisations Museum, Singapore

Bequest of Tony Wee and Colin Holland

粉彩凤凰牡丹纹盖盅

19世纪末至20世纪初

通高15.2厘米，口径12.1厘米

新加坡亚洲文明博物馆 藏

Famille-Rose Chupu with Phoenix and Peony Motifs

Late 19th to early 20th century

Total height 15.2 cm, mouth diameter 12.1 cm

Asian Civilisations Museum, Singapore

粉
彩
凤
凰
牡
丹
纹
盘

清宣统年间
高2.8厘米，口径19.9厘米
新加坡亚洲文明博物馆 藏

Famille-Rose Plate with Phoenix and Peony Motifs
Qing Dynasty, Xuantong period
Height 2.8 cm, mouth diameter 19.9 cm
Asian Civilisations Museum, Singapore

粉彩凤凰牡丹纹碗

19世纪末至20世纪初
高7.3厘米，口径16.2厘米
新加坡亚洲文明博物馆 藏

Famille-Rose Bowl with Phoenix and Peony Motifs
Late 19th to early 20th century
Height 7.3 cm, mouth diameter 16.2 cm
Asian Civilisations Museum, Singapore

粉彩凤凰牡丹纹碗

清光绪年间
高5.2厘米，口径10.8厘米
新加坡亚洲文明博物馆 藏

Famille-Rose Bowl with Phoenix and Peony Motifs
Qing Dynasty, Guangxu Period
Height 5.2 cm, mouth diameter 10.8 cm
Asian Civilisations Museum, Singapore

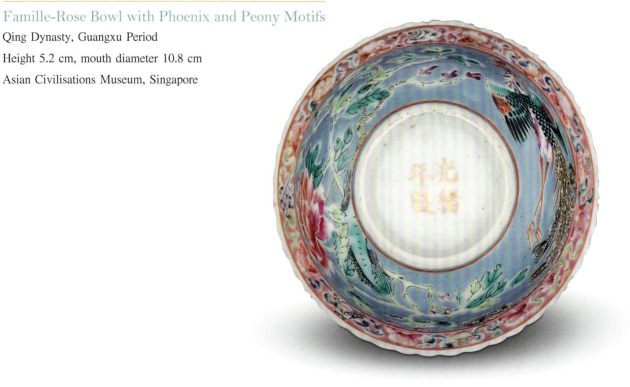

粉彩凤凰牡丹纹盖碗

清光绪年间

通高10.7厘米，口径16厘米

新加坡亚洲文明博物馆 藏

Tony Wee 和Colin Holland 遗赠

Famille-Rose Covered Bowl with Phoenix and Peony Motifs

Qing Dynasty, Guangxu Period

Total height 10.7 cm, mouth diameter 16 cm

Asian Civilisations Museum, Singapore

Bequest of Tony Wee and Colin Holland

英式粉彩凤凰牡丹纹茶壶

19世纪末至20世纪初

通高14厘米，口径6.5厘米

新加坡亚洲文明博物馆 藏

Tony Wee 和 Colin Holland 遗赠

English Style Famille-Rose Teapot with Phoenix and Peony Motifs

Late 19th to early 20th century

Total height 14 cm, mouth diameter 6.5 cm

Asian Civilisations Museum, Singapore

Bequest of Tony Wee and Colin Holland

欧洲人像（一对）

20世纪早期
A：长8.7厘米，宽7.9厘米，高26.5厘米
B：长9.9厘米，宽10厘米，高28.2厘米
新加坡土生文化馆 藏

European Figurines (Pair)

Early 20th century
A: Length 8.7 cm, width 7.9 cm, height 26.5 cm
B: Length 9.9 cm, width 10 cm, height 28.2 cm
Peranakan Museum, Singapore

欧洲陶瓷人像是很受欢迎的收藏品，通常展示在峇峇娘惹家庭的橱柜上。

European ceramic figurines are highly favored collectibles, typically displayed in the cabinets of Peranakan Nyonya households.

A   B

土生华人的物质文化反映了其受到诸多文化的影响。他们的家具包括以中国和欧洲为主题的柚木家具，并由中国工匠在东南亚地区制造。早期，土生华人喜欢用嵌螺钿装饰的黑檀家具，这种类型的家具是土生华人传统住宅待客厅中的一部分。

Elegant and Rich Peranakan Furniture

Peranakan material culture reflects the influence of many cultures. Their home furnishings include rich teak wood furniture featuring Chinese and European motifs, made in Southeast Asia by Chinese craftsmen. In the early days, Peranakans also favored Chinese *heitan* furniture adorned with mother-of-pearl inlay. This type of furniture was nearly always part of the formal receiving hall of the traditional Peranakan home.

酸枝嵌螺钿石芯扶手椅

民国

长62.5厘米，宽48.5厘米，高101厘米

中国（海南）南海博物馆 藏

Suanzhi Armchair with Inlaid Mother-of-Pearl and Jade Core

Republic of China

Length 62.5 cm, width 48.5 cm, height 101 cm

China (Hainan) Museum of the South China Sea

酸枝嵌螺钿石芯扶手椅

民国

长62.5厘米，宽47.8厘米，高101厘米

中国（海南）南海博物馆 藏

Suanzhi Armchair with Inlaid Mother-of-Pearl
and Jade Core

Republic of China

Length 62.5 cm, width 47.8 cm, height 101 cm

China (Hainan) Museum of the South China Sea

酸
枝
嵌
螺
钿
石
芯
扶
手
椅

民国

长62.3厘米，宽48厘米，高101厘米

中国（海南）南海博物馆 藏

Suanzhi Armchair with Inlaid Mother-of-
Pearl and Jade Core

Republic of China

Length 62.3 cm, width 48 cm, height 101 cm

China (Hainan) Museum of the South China Sea

民国

长62厘米，宽48.2厘米，高101厘米

中国（海南）南海博物馆 藏

Suanzhi Armchair with Inlaid Mother-of-
Pearl and Jade Core

Republic of China

Length 62 cm, width 48.2 cm, height 101 cm

China (Hainan) Museum of the South China Sea

民国

宽41厘米，高80厘米

中国（海南）南海博物馆 藏

Suanzhi Side Table with Inlaid Mother-
of-Pearl and Jade Core

Republic of China

Width 41 cm, height 80 cm

China (Hainan) Museum of the South China Sea

酸枝嵌螺钿石芯方几

民国
宽40.8厘米，高80厘米
中国（海南）南海博物馆 藏

Suanzhi Side Table with Inlaid Mother-
of-Pearl and Jade Core

Republic of China

Width 40.8 cm, height 80 cm

China (Hainan) Museum of the South China Sea

清代

长97厘米，宽48厘米，高99.5厘米

中国（海南）南海博物馆 藏

"Nanshenglong Zao" Crafted *Hongmu*
High Table with Inlaid Mother-of-Pearl
and Jade Surface

Qing Dynasty

Length 97 cm, width 48 cm, height 99.5 cm

China (Hainan) Museum of the South China Sea

红木嵌螺钿掐铜丝半圆桌（一对）

民国
高87.1厘米，直径104.3厘米
中国（海南）南海博物馆 藏

Hongmu Inlaid Mother-of-Pearl and Engraved
Copper Wire Semi-Circular Tables (Pair)
Republic of China
Height 87.1 cm, diameter 104.3 cm
China (Hainan) Museum of the South China Sea

酸枝嵌螺钿背屏
广绣花鸟图扶手椅

民国
长58厘米，宽71.2厘米，高98.8厘米
中国（海南）南海博物馆 藏

Suanzhi Armchair with Inlaid Mother-of-
Pearl Backrest Embroidered with Flower
and Bird Motifs
Republic of China
Length 58 cm, width 71.2 cm, height 98.8 cm
China (Hainan) Museum of the South China Sea

酸枝嵌螺钿背屏广绣花鸟图扶手椅

民国
长58.3厘米，宽72厘米，高98.6厘米
中国（海南）南海博物馆 藏

Suanzhi Armchair with Inlaid Mother-of-
Pearl Backrest Embroidered with Flower
and Bird Motifs
Republic of China
Length 58.3 cm, width 72 cm, height 98.6 cm
China (Hainan) Museum of the South China Sea

酸枝嵌螺钿『多子多福』鼓凳

清代

宽46厘米，高52厘米，面径37厘米

中国（海南）南海博物馆 藏

Suanzhi Drum Stool with Inlaid Mother-of-Pearl "Many Children, Many Blessings"

Qing Dynasty

Width 46 cm, height 52 cm, face diameter 37 cm

China (Hainan) Museum of the South China Sea

酸枝嵌螺钿『多子多福』鼓凳

清代

宽51厘米，高51.5厘米，面径36厘米

中国（海南）南海博物馆 藏

Suanzhi Drum Stool with Inlaid Mother-of-Pearl "Many Children, Many Blessings"

Qing Dynasty

Width 51 cm, height 51.5 cm, face diameter 36 cm

China (Hainan) Museum of the South China Sea

红木嵌螺钿花鸟图云石半圆桌

民国

高80.3厘米，直径91.3厘米

中国（海南）南海博物馆 藏

Hongmu Marble Semi-Circular Table with Inlaid Mother-of-Peal Flower and Bird Motifs

Republic of China

Height 80.3 cm, diameter 91.3 cm

China (Hainan) Museum of the South China Sea

三
中西相融的峇峇娘惹住宅建筑

19世纪初，新加坡成为英国殖民地。接受过西方教育的峇峇们凭借着家族商业背景与自身的语言优势，多被聘为贸易中间商，以开拓市场。在这样的背景下，西方文化的影响在峇峇娘惹的生活中日益凸显，在建筑、家居装饰上均有体现。

19世纪末，西欧和日本已迈入工业化制瓷的时代，欧式瓷砖就是这些地区工业瓷制品输入东南亚地区的缩影，较为均一的瓷砖尺寸也是工业化制瓷的结果。这些舶来瓷砖受19世纪末、20世纪初风靡欧洲的新艺术运动影响，注重自然元素和简洁的几何线条。

The Harmonious Blend of Eastern and Western Elements in the Architecture of Baba Nyonya Homes

In the early 19th century, Singapore became a British colony. The Babas, having received Western education, used their family's commercial background and linguistic skills to become key trade intermediaries, thus facilitating market expansion. Against this backdrop, the influence of Western culture became increasingly evident in the Baba Nyonya's way of life, particularly reflected in their architecture and home decor.

By the late 19th century, Western Europe and Japan had entered the era of industrial porcelain production. European style tiles represent the epitome of these industrial ceramic products imported into Southeast Asia. The relatively uniform size of the tiles is also a result of industrialized ceramic production. These imported tiles bear the influence of the Art Nouveau movement, which was popular in Europe at the end of the 19th century and the beginning of the 20th century, emphasizing natural elements and simple geometric lines.

欧式装饰瓷砖

European Style Decorative Tiles

19世纪末至20世纪初，大批量生产的、带有该时期新艺术风格的粉彩花卉图案瓷砖受到了海峡殖民地业主（包括土生华人）的青睐。他们用华丽的瓷砖装饰房屋的内部和外部。大部分瓷砖从英国进口，但也有些来自比利时、奥地利和日本。这种瓷砖风尚从他们房屋装饰延续到墓碑装饰。

During the late 19th and early 20th century, mass-produced tiles with pastel-coloured floral motifs in the Art Nouveau-style of the period, were favoured by homeowners in the Straits Settlements, including Chinese Peranakans. The interiors and exteriors of their homes were decorated with these ornate decorative tiles. Most were imported from the England, but they also came from Belgium, Austria, and Japan. The fashion for such tiles extended into the afterlife, with Chinese Peranakan grave markers featuring similar adornments.

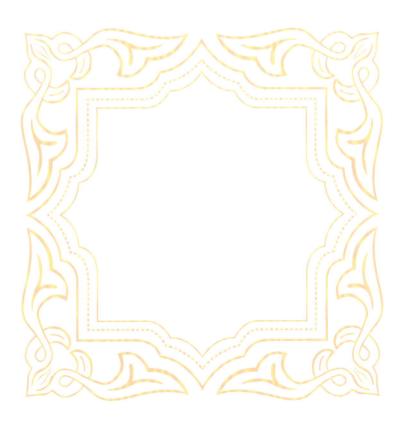

20世纪初

边长15.3厘米

新加坡亚洲文明博物馆 藏

Floral Patterned Square Tile

Early 20th century

Side length 15.3 cm

Asian Civilisations Museum, Singapore

花
卉
纹
方
砖

20世纪初

边长15.3厘米

新加坡亚洲文明博物馆 藏

Floral Patterned Square Tile

Early 20th century

Side length 15.3 cm

Asian Civilisations Museum, Singapore

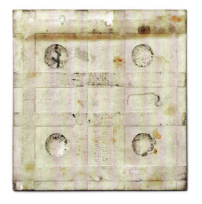

花
卉
纹
方
砖

20世纪初

边长15.5厘米

新加坡国家博物馆 藏

Floral Patterned Square Tile

Early 20th century

Side length 15.5 cm

National Museum of Singapore

C0988A

花
卉
纹
方
砖

20世纪初

边长15.2厘米

新加坡国家博物馆 藏

Floral Patterned Square Tile

Early 20th century

Side length 15.2 cm

National Museum of Singapore

20世纪初

边长15.2厘米

新加坡国家博物馆 藏

Floral Patterned Square Tile

Early 20th century

Side length 15.2 cm

National Museum of Singapore

带
四
块
花
砖
的
墓
志

1917年
边长15.3厘米
新加坡土生文化馆 藏
T. W. Ong家族 赠

Grave Marker with Four Floral Tiles
1917
Side length 15.3 cm
Peranakan Museum, Singapore
Gift of the family of T.W. Ong

这块墓志残片上有四块欧式花砖，是温深娘（1886—1917）墓的一部分。该墓原位于新加坡武吉布朗公墓，2014年因市政重建而被发掘。该墓尺寸接近16米×24米，是受影响最大的单人墓。墓的外围延展部分装饰的是带有粉色花卉图案的瓷砖，平台的地面上则装饰着马赛克瓷砖。

This grave marker fragment featuring four European floral tiles was part of the tomb of Oon Chim Neo (1886—1917). Originally located in Bukit Brown Cemetery, Singapore, the grave was exhumed in 2014 to facilitate municipal redevelopment. At almost 16 by 24 metres, her grave was the largest single person tomb affected. Tiles with pastel-coloured floral motifs decorated the arms of the tomb, while mosaic tiles decorated the floor of the tomb terrace.

第三单元

Unit 3

多元文化融合的信仰

海上贸易的发展及多元文化间的交流与影响，使得峇峇娘惹社区所奉行的信仰也呈现出多元性的特点。

Beliefs Shaped by
Multi-Cultural Integration

The spread of maritime trade and cross-cultural interactions have enriched the Baba-Nyonya community's religious landscape, showcasing a diversity of beliefs.

受中华文化影响的传统信仰

传统而言，土生华人信奉道教、佛教、儒教、中国民间信仰或祖先崇拜，他们从家族中来自中国南方的祖先身上传承了这些习俗。随着时间的推移，土生华人社区也吸收了东南亚本土社群的信仰与习俗。

Traditional Beliefs Influenced by Chinese Culture

Traditionally, Chinese Peranakans practised a range of Daoism, Buddhism, Confucianism, folk beliefs, and ancestor worship. These practices were inherited from their ancestors in southern China. Over time, beliefs and customs from the local communities have been incorporated into the rites and rituals of Peranakans.

土生华人家中的供桌
Altars in Chinese Peranakan Homes

土生华人家中通常有三个供桌，分别供奉家神、祖先和灶神。家神供桌一般设在正对大门的会客厅，以保护房屋和家人免受厄运和邪灵的侵扰。土生华人供奉的神灵包括佛教的观音菩萨，或道教的关公、张飞和刘备。家庭成员每日都会祈祷。供桌上会摆放各种食物和饮料，并装饰花卉，前面还会挂着一面桌帏（tok wi）。

Chinese Peranakan homes would typically have three altars-dedicated to the household deity, the ancestors, and the kitchen god. The household deity altar was usually in the main reception hall, facing the main entrance, in order to protect the house and its inhabitants from bad luck and evil spirits. The deities venerated by Chinese Peranakans included the Buddhist Goddess of Mercy Guanyin, or the deities of popular Daoism Guan Gong, Zhang Fei and Liu Bei. Family members would offer prayers daily. An assortment of food and drink would be displayed on the altar as offerings, along with floral decorations. An altar cloth (tok wi) was hung at the front of the altar.

陈金殿家族住宅『Botan House』会客厅的供桌

19世纪末至20世纪初，新加坡

纵29.6厘米，横23.7厘米

明胶银盐印相

Altar in the Reception Hall of "Botan House", Family Home of Tan Kim Tian
Late 19th to early 20th century, Singapore

Height 29.6 cm, width 23.7 cm

Gelatin silver print

福禄寿三星桌帏

19世纪末至20世纪初

长107.6厘米，宽101厘米

新加坡亚洲文明博物馆 藏

Altar Cloth with Three Stellar Gods Hock Lock Siew (*Fu Lu Shou*)

Late 19th to early 20th century

Length 107.6 cm, width 101 cm

Asian Civilisations Museum, Singapore

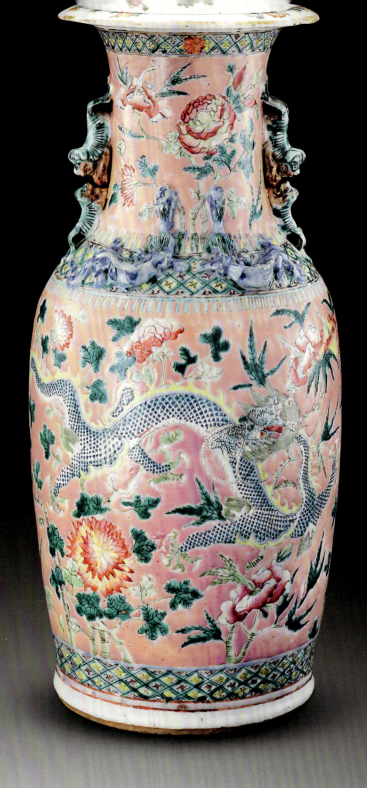

粉彩龙纹双耳瓶

清光绪年间

高45.2厘米，口径17.3厘米

新加坡亚洲文明博物馆 藏

Famille-Rose Double-Ear
Vase with Dragon Motif

Qing Dynasty, Guangxu period

Height 45.2 cm, mouth diameter 17.3 cm

Asian Civilisations Museum, Singapore

粉彩凤凰牡丹纹盘

清光绪年间
长18.2厘米，宽9.6厘米，高1.5厘米
新加坡亚洲文明博物馆 藏

Famille-Rose Tray with Phoenix and Peony Motifs
Qing Dynasty, Guangxu period
Length 18.2 cm, width 9.6 cm, height 1.5 cm
Asian Civilisations Museum, Singapore

粉彩牡丹纹杯

清光绪年间
高3.6厘米，口径6.6厘米
新加坡亚洲文明博物馆 藏

Famille-Rose Cup with Peony Motif
Qing Dynasty, Guangxu period
Height 3.6 cm, mouth diameter 6.6 cm
Asian Civilisations Museum, Singapore

粉彩牡丹纹杯

清光绪年间
高3.5厘米，口径6.7厘米
新加坡亚洲文明博物馆 藏

Famille-Rose Cup with Peony Motif
Qing Dynasty, Guangxu period
Height 3.5 cm, mouth diameter 6.7 cm
Asian Civilisations Museum, Singapore

粉
彩
牡
丹
纹
杯

清光绪年间
高3.5厘米，口径6.7厘米
新加坡亚洲文明博物馆 藏

Famille-Rose Cup with Peony Motif
Qing Dynasty, Guangxu period
Height 3.5 cm, mouth diameter 6.7 cm
Asian Civilisations Museum, Singapore

黄铜烛台（一对）

19世纪末至20世纪初

高37.2厘米，盘径19厘米

新加坡亚洲文明博物馆 藏

Brass Candlesticks (Pair)

Late 19th to early 20th century

Height 37.2 cm, diameter 19 cm

Asian Civilisations Museum, Singapore

纹香筒

**Famille-Rose Cylindrical Incense
Holder with Peony Motif**

Qing Dynasty, Guangxu period

Height 23.3 cm, mouth diameter 8.6 cm

Asian Civilisations Museum, Singapore

楠木描金雕龙纹烛台（一对）

19世纪末至20世纪初
高56厘米，底径13厘米
新加坡亚洲文明博物馆 藏

Nanmu Gilt-Carved Dragon-Patterned
Candlesticks (Pair)
Late 19th to early 20th century
Height 56 cm, bottom diameter 13 cm
Asian Civilisations Museum, Singapore

粉彩凤凰牡丹纹盘（5件）

1911—1930年

A：高2.5厘米，口径19.6厘米

B：高3厘米，口径19.7厘米

C：高2.8厘米，口径19.5厘米

D：高2.5厘米，口径19.5厘米

E：高2.5厘米，口径19.5厘米

新加坡土生文化馆 藏

由新加坡亚洲文明博物馆之友通过2009年晚宴筹得的资金购置

Famille-Rose Plates with Phoenix and Peony Motifs (Set of 5)

1911—1930

A: Height 2.5 cm, mouth diameter 19.6 cm

B: Height 3 cm, mouth diameter 19.7 cm

C: Height 2.8 cm, mouth diameter 19.5 cm

D: Height 2.5 cm, mouth diameter 19.5 cm

E: Height 2.5 cm, mouth diameter 19.5 cm

Peranakan Museum, Singapore

Acquired with funds from Friends of ACM through Gala Dinner 2009

A

B

C

D

E

黑漆描金山水纹祭品盒

20世纪初

长35厘米，宽15厘米，高26.3厘米

新加坡土生文化馆 藏

Black Lacquer with Gold-Painted Landscape Patterned Offering

Early 20th century

Length 35 cm, width 15 cm, height 26.3 cm

Peranakan Museum, Singapore

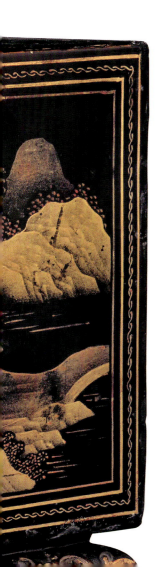

黄
铜
灯

19世纪末至20世纪初

高36厘米

新加坡国家博物馆 藏

Brass Lamp

Late 19th to early 20th century

Height 36 cm

National Museum of Singapore

香炉

20世纪初

长40厘米，宽15厘米，高21.5厘米

新加坡国家博物馆 藏

Incense Burner

Early 20th century

Length 40 cm, width 15 cm, height 21.5 cm

National Museum of Singapore

粉彩凤凰牡丹纹香炉

19世纪末至20世纪初

高11.6厘米，口径12.5厘米

新加坡土生文化馆 藏

Sunny Chan Hean Kee 赠

Famille-Rose Incense Burner with Phoenix and Peony Motifs

Late 19th to early 20th century

Height 11.6 cm, mouth diameter 12.5 cm

Peranakan Museum, Singapore

Gift of Sunny Chan Hean Kee

1911—1930年

通高8.5厘米，底径6厘米

新加坡土生文化馆 藏

Tony Wee 和 Colin Holland 遗赠

Famille-Rose Teapot with Flower Motif

1911—1930

Total height 8.5 cm, bottom diameter 6 cm

Peranakan Museum, Singapore

Bequest of Tony Wee and Colin Holland

20世纪50—60年代

长26.3厘米，宽22.5厘米，高51厘米

新加坡土生文化馆 藏

楠木彩绘描金关公像

Nanmu Painted and Gilded Statue of Guan Gong

1950s—1960s

Length 26.3 cm, width 22.5 cm, height 51 cm

Peranakan Museum, Singapore

19世纪末

长51.6厘米，宽52.7厘米，高109厘米

新加坡亚洲文明博物馆 藏

Nanmu Lacquered and Gilded Lantern Dedicated to Tian Gong (Jade Emperor)

late 19th century

Length 51.6 cm, width 52.7 cm, height 109 cm

Asian Civilisations Museum, Singapore

天公（玉皇大帝）是受峇峇娘惹崇拜的最重要的神之一，他们祖宅的正门前醒目地悬挂着天公灯笼。峇峇娘惹会在天公生日（农历正月初九）当天，用精心制作的食物和纸来庆祝。这个特别大的天公灯笼很可能挂在如寺庙等公共建筑前。

The Tian Gong (Jade Emperor) is one of the most revered deities worshiped by the Peranakan Chinese. A prominent Tian Gong lantern hangs conspicuously in front of the main entrance of the Peranakan ancestral home. On the Tian Gong's birthday (the 9th day of the first month of Chinese calendar), the Peranakan Chinese celebrate with carefully crafted food and paper offerings. This large and distinctive Tian Gong lantern is likely displayed in front of a public building such as a temple.

19世纪末至20世纪初

长61厘米，宽45.5厘米，高71厘米

新加坡土生文化馆 藏

Nanmu Gold-Painted Carved Spirit House
for Ancestral Tablets

Late 19th to early 20th century

Length 61 cm, width 45.5 cm, height 71 cm

Peranakan Museum, Singapore

朱漆牌位

20世纪初
长21厘米，宽10.5厘米，高37.5厘米
新加坡国家博物馆 藏

Lacquered Ancestral Tablet
Early 20th century
Length 21 cm, width 10.5 cm, height 37.5 cm
National Museum of Singapore

龙纹桌帏

20世纪早期至中期
长108厘米，宽103厘米
新加坡土生文化馆 藏
Rudolf G. Smend 赠

Dragon-Patterned Altar Cloth
Early to mid-20th century
Length 108 cm, width 103 cm
Peranakan Museum, Singapore
Gift of Rudolf G. Smend

这块桌帏上写有"慎终追远"四个字，意为慎重地办理亲人丧事，虔诚地祭祀远代祖先，引申开来，提醒人们勿忘先人。

This altar cloth is inscribed with the words *"Shenzhongzhuiyuan"*, meaning to conscientiously handle the affairs of the deceased, devoutly offering sacrifices to ancestors from distant generations. In a broader sense, it serves as a reminder not to forget one's forebears.

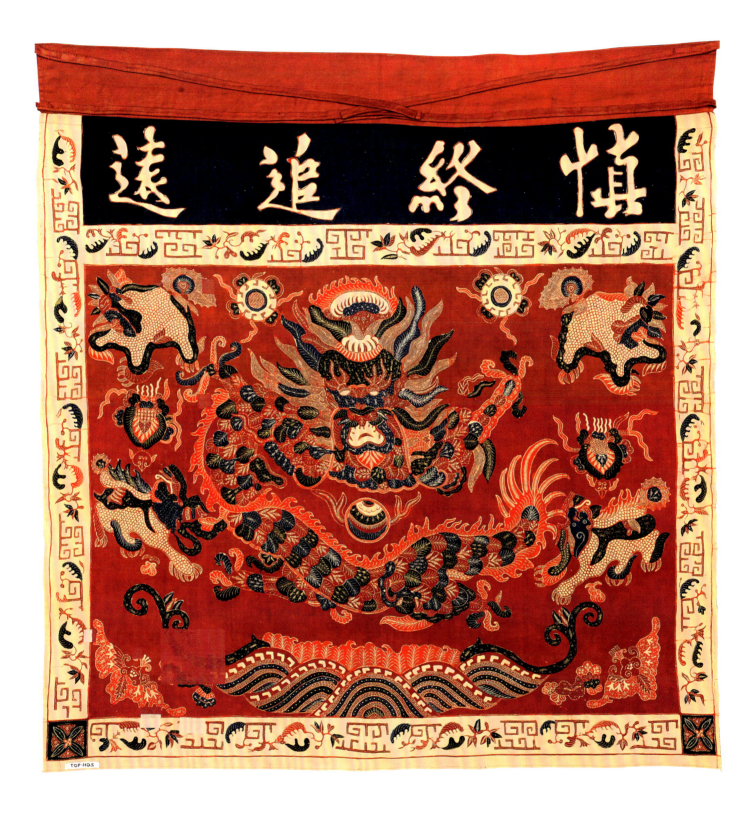

二 多元文化影响下的信仰

海上贸易促成的社会多元化发展，促使峇峇娘惹社区的信仰也趋于多元化。许多峇峇娘惹信奉基督教，土生印度人信奉印度教，土生爪哇和阿拉伯人则信奉伊斯兰教。

Beliefs Under the Influence of a Multicultural Society

The enhancement of social diversity through maritime trade has led to a diversification of faiths within the Baba-Nyonya community. Many Baba Nyonya have converted to Christianity. Many Indian Peranakans are Hindus, while Jawi and Arab Peranakans are followers of Islam.

银质哀悼珠宝套装

19世纪末至20世纪初

新加坡亚洲文明博物馆 藏

Edmond Chin先生 赠

Silver Mourning Jewelry Set
Late 19th to early 20th century
Asian Civilisations Museum, Singapore
Gift of Mr Edmond Chin

不同土生家庭的哀悼期也不一样，可能会持续几个月到三年左右。哀悼期的娘惹们会把她们的黄金和钻石珠宝收起来，转而戴上银、珍珠、绿色或蓝色的宝石。

Depending on the family, the mourning period for Peranakan households may last from a few months to around three years. During the mourning period, the Nyonyas would set aside their gold and diamond jewelry and instead wear silver, pearls, and gemstones in green or blue.

銀
鍍
金
护
身
符
19世纪末至20世纪初

长3.9厘米，宽2.6厘米

新加坡亚洲文明博物馆 藏

———————————

Silver-Gilt Amulet

Late 19th to early 20th century

Length 3.9 cm, width 2.6 cm

银镀金观音护身符

19世纪末至20世纪初
长4.5厘米，宽6厘米
新加坡土生文化馆 藏
Wee Liu Kim夫人 赠

Silver-Gilt Guanyin Amulet
Late 19th to early 20th century
Length 4.5 cm, width 6 cm
Peranakan Museum, Singapore
Gift of Mdm Wee Liu Kim

银镶珍珠哀悼胸针

19世纪末至20世纪初
长5.3厘米，宽5.7厘米
新加坡亚洲文明博物馆 藏
Edmond Chin 先生 赠

Silver and Pearl Mourning Brooch
Late 19th to early 20th century
Length 5.3 cm, width 5.7 cm
Asian Civilisations Museum, Singapore
Gift of Mr Edmond Chin

这枚有狮子和独角兽图案的哀悼胸针，其设计很可能是受到了英国国徽的启发。

The design of this mourning period brooch, featuring a lion and a unicorn, is likely inspired by the United Kingdom royal coat of arms.

第四单元

Unit 4

中西结合的婚俗文化

峇峇娘惹的婚俗文化保留了大量华人的传统习俗。与中国传统婚姻观一样，峇峇娘惹们十分讲究"门当户对"，有权有势的华人首领、富商家族之间经常联姻。

The Marriage Culture Integrating Chinese and Western Elements

The marriage customs of the Baba-Nyonya community retain numerous traditional Chinese practices. Echoing traditional Chinese views on marriage, the Baba-Nyonya place a high value on marriages that are well-matched, with alliances often formed between powerful Chinese leaders and affluent business families.

中西融合的婚仪

峇峇娘惹们接触着西方文化，也受到马来文化的影响，又保留着古老的华人传统和习惯，这使得他们在婚俗仪礼的传承中兼容发展，多元融合。

Wedding Ceremony Integrating Chinese and Western Elements

Influenced by Western culture, shaped by Malay customs, and still holding onto ancient Chinese traditions and practices, the Baba-Nyonya community has evolved a wedding ceremony practice that exemplifies a rich fusion of cultural elements.

刺绣腰包

19世纪末至20世纪初

长11厘米，宽10.5厘米

新加坡国家博物馆 藏

Embroidered Belt Purse (o pau)

late 19th to early 20th century

Length 11cm, width 10.5 cm

National Museum of Singapore

　　这件钱包是仿照清代流行的中国刺绣荷包设计而成。在海峡殖民地，交换结婚礼物通常包括给新郎的腰包，新郎和新娘在梳头仪式上也会佩戴腰包。

This purse is inspired by the popular embroidered lotus purses from the Qing Dynasty in China. In the Straits Settlements, exchanging wedding gifts often included presenting a belt purse to the groom. Both the bride and groom would also wear a belt purse during the hair-combing ceremony.

19世纪末至20世纪初
长44.5厘米，宽10厘米
新加坡亚洲文明博物馆 藏
Edmond Chin先生 赠

Silver-Gilt Filigree Wedding Necklace

late 19th to early 20th century
Length 44.5 cm, width 10 cm
Asian Civilisations Museum, Singapore
Gift of Mr Edmond Chin

马六甲、新加坡和爪哇的土生华人新娘戴的项链采用花丝工艺的饰板，中间由链条连接。它们被称为 rantai papan（马来语"饰板项链"），新婚的马来夫妇也会佩戴这种项链。

Necklaces worn by Peranakan brides of Chinese descent in Malacca, Singapore, and Java feature ornamental plates crafted with filigree work, connected by chains in the middle. Called rantai papan ("plank neck-chain" in Malay), these intricately designed pieces are also worn by newlywed Malay couples.

约20世纪30年代

纵23.4厘米，横29.2厘米

新加坡土生文化馆 藏

Lee Kip Lee夫妇 赠

土生婚礼新人和男女花童

Peranakan Wedding Couple with Page Boy and Page Girl

Around 1930s

Height 23.4 cm, width 29.2 cm

Peranakan Museum, Singapore

Gift of Mr and Mrs Lee Kip Lee

土生婚礼新人

约20世纪20年代
纵45.6厘米，横35.2厘米
新加坡土生文化馆 藏
Lee Kip Lee夫妇 赠

Peranakan Wedding Couple
Around 1920s
Height 45.6 cm, width 35.2 cm
Peranakan Museum, Singapore
Gift of Mr and Mrs Lee Kip Lee

穿西式婚服的土生
新郎 Ong Hay Way 和
新娘 Thio Chan Bee

1927年

纵15.7厘米，横20.7厘米

新加坡土生文化馆 藏

Lee Kip Lee夫妇 赠

Peranakan Bride and Groom Thio Chan Bee & Ong Hay Way in Western Wedding Attire

1927

Height 15.7 cm, width 20.7 cm

Peranakan Museum, Singapore

Gift of Mr and Mrs Lee Kip Lee

粉彩凤凰牡丹纹盖罐

19世纪末至20世纪初

通高14.5厘米，底径12厘米

新加坡亚洲文明博物馆 藏

Famille-Rose Kamcheng with Phoenix and Peony Motifs

Late 19th to early 20th century

Total height 14.5 cm, bottom diameter 12 cm

Asian Civilisations Museum, Singapore

正式举行婚礼仪式前，峇峇娘惹的新娘新郎须互送汤圆，且新人必须一口吃下红白共两颗汤圆，不可咀嚼，须直接吞下，喻意喜庆甜蜜和白头偕老。

Before the formal wedding ceremony, Peranakan brides and grooms must exchange glutinous rice balls. The newlyweds are required to simultaneously consume one red and one white glutinous rice ball without chewing, symbolizing the joyous sweetness of marriage and the wish for a lifelong union. The distinctive Peranakan dishes served during the wedding are indispensable culinary delights in Peranakan Nyonya weddings.

银镀金槟榔盒

约1950年

长17厘米，宽12.5厘米，高6.5厘米

新加坡土生文化馆 藏

纪念万鸦老Tan Tjien Sian家族的捐赠

Tortoiseshell Silver-Gilt Betel Nut Box

Approximately 1950

Length 17 cm, width 12.5 cm, height 6.5 cm

Peranakan Museum, Singapore

Gift in memory of Family Tan Tjien Sian, Manado

清光緒年間
高13厘米，口径18厘米
新加坡亚洲文明博物馆 藏
Tony Wee 和 Colin Holland 遗赠

Famille-Rose Spittoon with Floral Pattern
Framed Panels and Made in the Guangxu
Reign of the Great Qing Dynasty Mark
Qing Dynasty, Guangxu Period
Height 13 cm, mouth diameter 18 cm
Asian Civilisations Museum, Singapore
Bequest of Tony Wee and Colin Holland

清光绪年间
高13厘米，口径18厘米
新加坡亚洲文明博物馆 藏

134

餐垫

19世纪末至20世纪初

长38.8厘米，宽30.3厘米

新加坡土生文化馆 藏

Table Mat

Late 19th to early 20th century

Length 38.8 cm, width 30.3 cm

Peranakan Museum, Singapore

男士拖鞋

20世纪初
长25.5厘米，宽9.5厘米，高5.8厘米
新加坡土生文化馆 藏

Men's Slippers

Early 20th century
Length 25.5cm, width 9.5 cm, height 5.8 cm
Peranakan Museum, Singapore

在槟城、马六甲和新加坡，新人在交换结婚礼物时，新郎会收到金丝银线绣制的拖鞋，这种拖鞋被认为比珠绣拖鞋更正式，只有在特殊场合才会穿。

In Penang, Malacca, and Singapore, during the exchange of wedding gifts, the groom often receives intricately embroidered slippers adorned with gold and silver. These slippers are considered more formal than those embellished with beads and are reserved for special occasions.

20世纪初

长27.5厘米，宽9.7厘米，高5.6厘米

新加坡国家博物馆 藏

Men's Slippers

Early 20th century

Length 27.5 cm, width 9.7 cm, height 5.6 cm

National Museum of Singapore

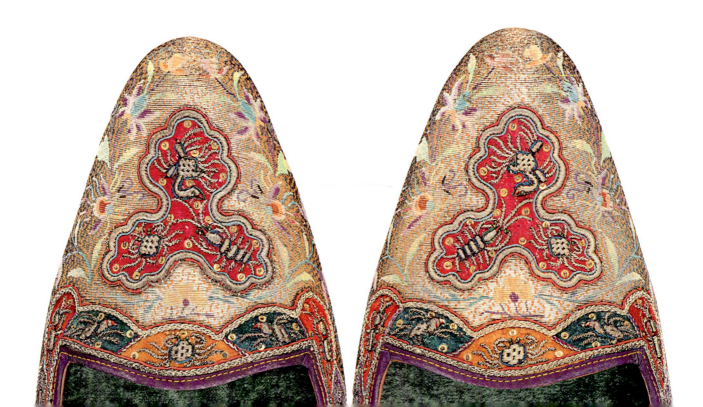

138

男士拖鞋

20世纪初

长23.5厘米，宽8.4厘米，高4.3厘米

新加坡国家博物馆 藏

Men's Slippers

Early 20th century

Length 23.5 cm, width 8.4 cm, height 4.3 cm

National Museum of Singapore

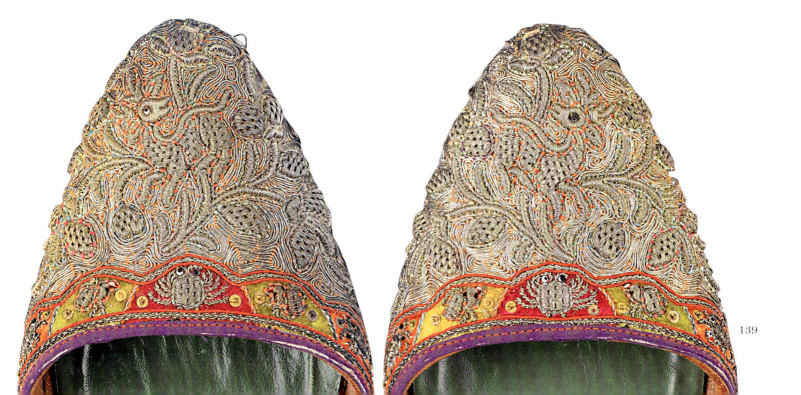

隆重的婚礼仪式

婚礼是峇峇娘惹一生中最隆重最讲究的礼仪之一。传统婚礼的程序十分复杂，要12天才能礼成。第二次世界大战前，峇峇娘惹的婚礼沿用清朝古礼：跪拜叩头（表示毕恭毕敬）、敲锣打鼓、抬花轿等，场面十分热闹。

Magnificent Wedding Ceremony

Weddings are among the most grandiose and elaborate ceremonies in the Baba-Nyonya community's lifetime. The procedure for a traditional wedding is intricate, requiring up to 12 days to conclude. Before the Second World War, Baba-Nyonya weddings retained ancient rituals from the Qing Dynasty, characterized by kneelings and kowtowing (a gesture symbolizing deep respect), musical accompaniment, and the procession of carrying bridal sedans, all contributing to a lively and festive atmosphere.

土生华人婚礼
叶福兴夫妇结婚照

约20世纪30年代，槟城

银盐照片

纵20.2厘米，横14.6厘米

新加坡土生文化馆 藏

Lee Kip Lee夫妇 赠

Wedding Portrait of Mr and Mrs Yeap Hock Hin

Around 1930s, Penang

Gelatin silver print

Height 20.2 cm, width 14.6 cm

Peranakan Museum, Singapore

Gift of Mr and Mrs Lee Kip Lee

描金镂雕花婚床

20世纪早期至中期
长230厘米，宽147.8厘米，高235厘米
新加坡土`生文化馆 藏

Elaborately Gilded and Carved Wedding Bed

Early to mid-20th century
Length 230 cm, width 147.8 cm, height 235 cm
Peranakan Museum, Singapore

此床和完整的床品属于Sharron Chee Guek Kee 家族。自20世纪起，它们至少五次用于在马六甲举办的婚礼。该家族是马六甲和新加坡有记载的最古老的土生华人家族之一，其早期祖先于18世纪初从中国福建移居至此。

The beds on display, along with their complete textiles, belonged to the family of Sharron Chee Guek Kee. They were used for at least five weddings in Malacca beginning in the early 20th century. The Chee family is one of the oldest documented Chinese Peranakan families in Malacca and Singapore. An early ancestor migrated from Fujian province, China, in the early 18th century.

绣花床挂（一对）

20世纪早期
高125厘米，宽16厘米
新加坡亚洲文明博物馆 藏
Edmond Chin先生 赠

Embroidered Bed Hanging Ornaments (Pair)
Early 20th century
Height 125 cm, width 16 cm
Asian Civilisations Museum, Singapore
Gift of Mr Edmond Chin

土生新人在婚床前面悬挂吉祥的挂饰，希望能获得好运和平安。

Peranakans hang auspicious decorations in front of the wedding bed, aiming to garner good fortune and peace.

花
卉
纹
窗
帘
钩
（
一
对
）

19世纪末至20世纪初

A：长24.2厘米，宽10.6厘米，高3.2厘米

B：长24.5厘米，宽10.6厘米，高3.2厘米

新加坡亚洲文明博物馆 藏

Edmond Chin先生 赠

Floral Patterned Curtain Hooks (Pair)

Late 19th to early 20th century

A: Length 24.2 cm, width 10.6 cm, height 3.2 cm

B: Length 24.5 cm, width 10.6 cm, height 3.2 cm

Asian Civilisations Museum, Singapore

Gift of Mr Edmond Chin

A

B

20世纪早期至中期

长211厘米，宽83.6厘米

新加坡土生文化馆 藏

凤
凰
牡
丹
纹
单
人
床
罩

Single Bed Cover with Phoenix and Peony Motifs

Early to mid-20th century

Length 211 cm, width 83.6 cm

Peranakan Museum, Singapore

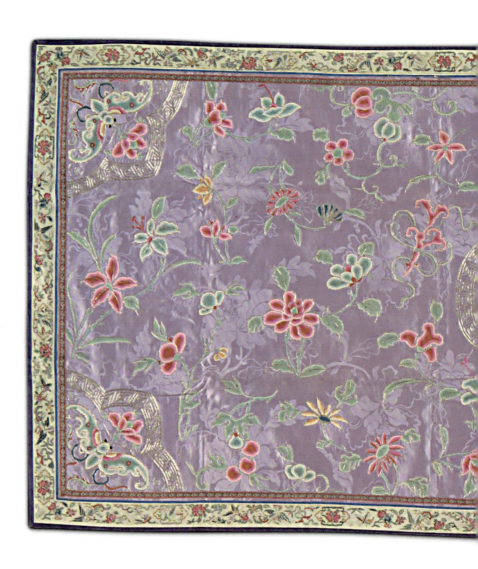

凤
凰
牡
丹
纹
双
人
床
罩

20世纪早期至中期

长211.4厘米，宽145.5厘米

新加坡土生文化馆 藏

Double Bed Cover with Phoenix and Peony Motifs

Early to mid-20th century

Length 211.4 cm, width 145.5 cm

Peranakan Museum, Singapore

20世纪早期

长44厘米，宽26.5厘米

新加坡亚洲文明博物馆 藏

Edmond Chin先生 赠

Floral Patterned Beaded Pillow Cover

Early 20th century

Length 44 cm, width 26.5 cm

Asian Civilisations Museum, Singapore

Gift of Mr Edmond Chin

这款珠绣枕巾的设计灵感来自欧洲的针绣花边图案。它很可能是用来装饰土生新人的婚床。

This beaded pillowcase is inspired by European needlepoint patterns and is likely designed to adorn the Peranakan wedding bed.

绣
花
鸟
兽
纹
床
帘

20世纪早期至中期
长840厘米，宽218厘米
新加坡土生文化馆 藏

Embroidered Bed Curtain with Bird
and Animal Motifs
Early to mid-20th century
Length 840 cm, width 218 cm
Peranakan Museum, Singapore

绣花鸟兽纹床帘（一对）

20世纪早期至中期

A：长211厘米，宽86.4厘米

B：长211厘米，宽86.2厘米

新加坡土生文化馆 藏

Embroidered Bed Curtains with Bird and Animal Motifs (Pair)

Early to mid-20th century

A: Length 211 cm, width 86.4 cm

B: Length 211 cm, width 86.2 cm

Peranakan Museum, Singapore

A

绣花鸟兽纹帷幔（一对）

20世纪早期至中期

A：长88厘米，宽58.2厘米

B：长87.5厘米，宽57厘米

新加坡土生文化馆 藏

Embroidered Bed Hangings
with Bird and Animal Motifs (Pair)

Early to mid-20th century

A: Length 88 cm, width 58.2 cm

B: Length 87.5 cm, width 57 cm

Peranakan Museum, Singapore

B

163

花
卉
纹
床
帘
带
（
一
对
）

20世纪早期至中期
A：长22.5厘米，宽16.2厘米
B：长25厘米，宽16.2厘米
新加坡土生文化馆 藏

Floral Patterned Bed Curtain Ties (Pair)

Early to mid-20th century
A: Length 22.5 cm，width 16.2 cm
B: Length 25 cm，width 16.2 cm
Peranakan Museum, Singapore

A

B

绣花床垫边框（一对）

20世纪早期至中期

A：长237.5厘米，宽24.4厘米

B：长240厘米，宽24.5厘米

新加坡土生文化馆 藏

Embroidered Bed Mattress Borders with
Flower Motif (Pair)

Early to mid-20th century

A: Length 237.5 cm, width 24.4 cm

B: Length 240 cm, width 24.5 cm

Peranakan Museum, Singapore

A

B

20世纪早期至中期

A：长96.5厘米，宽58厘米

B：长96.5厘米，宽58.6厘米

新加坡土生文化馆 藏

Embroidered Bed Hangings with
Bird and Animal Motifs (Pair)

Early to mid-20th century

A: Length 96.5 cm, width 58 cm

B: Length 96.5 cm, width 58.6 cm

Peranakan Museum, Singapore

A

B

20世纪

长44厘米，宽15厘米

新加坡亚洲文明博物馆 藏

Beaded Decorative Cloth with Bird and Animal Motifs

20th century

Length 44 cm, width 15 cm

Asian Civilisations Museum, Singapore

这块布很可能是婚床的枕套。两端各有一只凤凰和麒麟，四周是水果、鲜花和金鱼，中间的圆饰图案有凤凰、蝴蝶、鸭子和鹿——象征着婚姻幸福、好运、忠诚和长寿。

This decorative cloth is likely a pillowcase for a wedding bed. Phoenixes and kylin appear at both ends, surrounded by fruits, flowers, and goldfish. In the central round motif, there are representations of phoenixes, butterflies, ducks, and deer, symbolizing marital happiness, good fortune, loyalty, and longevity.

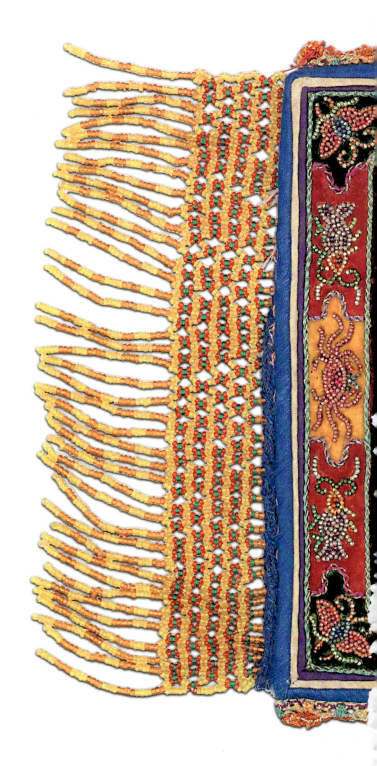

绣
花
鸟
兽
纹
床
挂
（
一
对
）

20世纪早期至中期

A：长13.5厘米，宽113.7厘米

B：长13.5厘米，宽113.2厘米

新加坡土生文化馆 藏

Embroidered Bed Hangings with Bird and Animal Motifs (Pair)

Early to mid-20th century

A: Length 13.5 cm, width 113.7 cm

B: Length 13.5 cm, width 113.2 cm

Peranakan Museum, Singapore

A

B

绣花枕头边

19世纪末至20世纪初
长31厘米，宽22.9厘米
新加坡土生文化馆 藏

Embroidered Pillow Ends
Late 19th to early 20th century
Length 31 cm, width 22.9 cm
Peranakan Museum, Singapore

Silver-Gilt *Qilin* and Miscellaneous Treasures Motifs Pillow Ends (Pair)

Late 19th to early 20th century

A: Length 14.5 cm, width 9 cm

B: Length 14.5 cm, width 9.1 cm

Asian Civilisations Museum, Singapore

A

银质花鸟纹枕头两端（一对）

20世纪早期

直径8.3厘米，厚1.9厘米

新加坡亚洲文明博物馆 藏

Edmond Chin先生 赠

Silver Flower and Bird Motifs Pillow Ends
(Pair)

Early 20th century

Diameter 8.3 cm, thickness 1.9 cm

Asian Civilisations Museum, Singapore

Gift of Mr Edmond Chin

20世纪早期

A：长16.5厘米，宽17厘米，厚0.1厘米

B：长17厘米，宽17厘米，厚0.1厘米

新加坡亚洲文明博物馆 藏

Edmond Chin先生 赠

Silver-Gilt *Qilin* and Butterfly Motifs Pillow Ends (Pair)

Early 20th century

A: Length 16.5 cm, width 17 cm, thickness 0.1 cm

B: Length 17 cm, width 17 cm, thickness 0.1 cm

Asian Civilisations Museum, Singapore

Gift of Mr Edmond Chin

A   B

花卉纹爱尔兰地毯

20世纪早期
长76厘米，宽76厘米
新加坡亚洲文明博物馆 藏

Floral Patterned Irish Carpet
Early 20th century
Length 76 cm, width 76 cm
Asian Civilisations Museum, Singapore

　　"爱尔兰地毯"是这类纺织品的贸易术语，许多土生娘惹家庭会使用这种纺织品作为地毯或桌布，它们经常出现在峇峇娘惹夫妇的婚纱照中。

　　"Irish carpet" is a trade term for such textiles, and many Peranakan Nyonya families used these textiles as carpets or tablecloths. They are often featured in the wedding photos of Peranakan Nyonya couples.

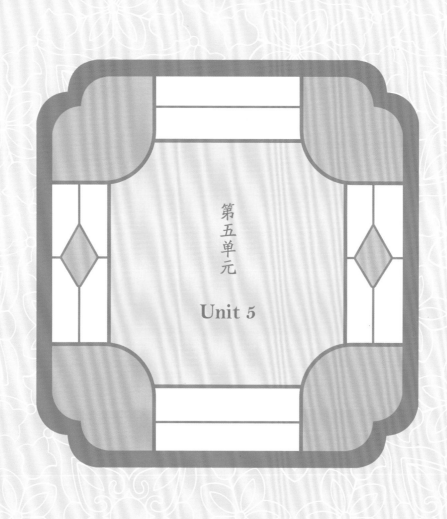

第五单元

Unit 5

传
统
与
现
代
的
娘
惹
时
尚

几个世纪以来，在东南亚港口城市的国际化环境中，娘惹时尚不断适应和发展，融合了各种不同因素的影响。它既混合多元，也不乏创新，在演变中坚持其恒久的、传统的核心价值，为亚洲传统时尚提供了新的视角。

Traditional and Contemporary Nyonya Fashion

Throughout centuries, the fashion of the Nyonya has adapted and thrived within the cosmopolitan environment of Southeast Asian port cities, assimilating a diverse array of influences. It stands out as both a blend and an innovation, offering new insights into Asian traditional fashion, which holds onto its core values of constancy and tradition amidst evolution.

一 风格独特的纱笼可峇雅

19世纪末20世纪初，许多土生女子穿着朴素但舒适的长衫。长衫搭配长裙布或者纱笼，纱笼最初是用从印度进口的棉纺织品制成。

大约在19世纪和20世纪之交，土生女子开始穿可峇雅（kebaya），这是一种宽松的长袖敞开式外套，用胸针（kerosang）固定衣襟，搭配峇迪纱笼穿着。从设计和形式上看，纱笼可峇雅是来源甚广的遗产。可峇雅最重要的元素源自古代伊斯兰世界早期的长袍（qaba）。20世纪初，较短的白色蕾丝可峇雅开始流行，这是荷属东印度群岛的欧亚女性的服装款式。到了20世纪30年代，可峇雅设计得更为贴身，通常用半透明的欧洲面料制作，有鸡心翻领和复杂的刺绣。裙布或纱笼由进口的印度棉纺织品制成，或者产于爪哇的峇迪生产中心（如拉森、井里汶和北加龙安）。

纱笼可峇雅是一种独特、优雅的服饰，已成为土生华人身份的象征，但长期以来，东南亚海/岛内许多不同社区的女性都穿着这种服饰，每个社区也形成了各自的风格。如今，许多土生女性在特殊场合仍然穿着纱笼可峇雅，可峇雅不断为新加坡、马来西亚和印度尼西亚的时尚注入灵感。

The Unique Style of Sarong Kebaya

In the late 19th and early 20th century, many Peranakan women wore the austere but comfortable baju panjang ("long tunic" in Malay). This was worn with a long skirt cloth or a sarong, which was originally made from imported Indian cotton textiles.

Around the turn of the 19th and 20th centuries, Peranakan women began wearing the kebaya, a loose long-sleeved open jacket fastened by brooches known as kerosang and paired with batik sarongs. In design and form, the sarong kebaya is a legacy of diverse sources. The top element, the kebaya, is derived from the ancient qaba, a robe worn in the early Islamic world. In the early 20th century, shorter white lace kebaya were popular, a style adopted from Eurasian women in the Dutch East Indies. By the 1930s, the kebaya was more form fitting, often made with translucent European fabrics, with tapered lapels and complex embroidery. The skirt cloths or sarongs were made from imported Indian cotton textiles or manufactured in the batik producing centres of Java such as Lasem, Cirebon, and Pekalongan.

The sarong kebaya is a distinctive, elegant outfit which has emerged as a symbol of Peranakan identity but has also long been worn by women of many different communities across maritime/insular Southeast Asia, with each community developing its own style. Today, many Peranakan women still wear sarong kebaya for special occasions and kebaya style continues to inspire Singaporean, Malaysian and Indonesian fashion.

印度棉手工木刻印花长衫

19世纪末

两袖通长166.6厘米，衣长113.5厘米

新加坡亚洲文明博物馆 藏

Lee Kip Lee夫妇 赠

Block Printed Indian Trade Cotton Baju Panjang

Late 19th century

Full-length straight sleeves 166.6 cm, total length (back neck to hem) 113.5 cm

Asian Civilisations Museum, Singapore

Gift of Mr and Mrs Lee Kip Lee

189

19世纪末至20世纪初

两袖通长146.5厘米，衣长121.5厘米

新加坡土生文化馆 藏

Lee Kip Lee夫妇 赠

Batik Baju Panjang

Late 19th to early 20th century

Full-length straight sleeves 146.5 cm, total length (back neck
to hem) 121.5 cm

Peranakan Museum, Singapore

Gift of Mr and Mrs Lee Kip Lee

191

18世纪

长351厘米，宽113.5厘米

新加坡亚洲文明博物馆 藏

Roger Hollander旧藏

Painted and Block Printed Skirt Fabric

18th century

Length 351 cm, width 113.5 cm

Asian Civilisations Museum, Singapore

Previously in the Roger Hollander Collection

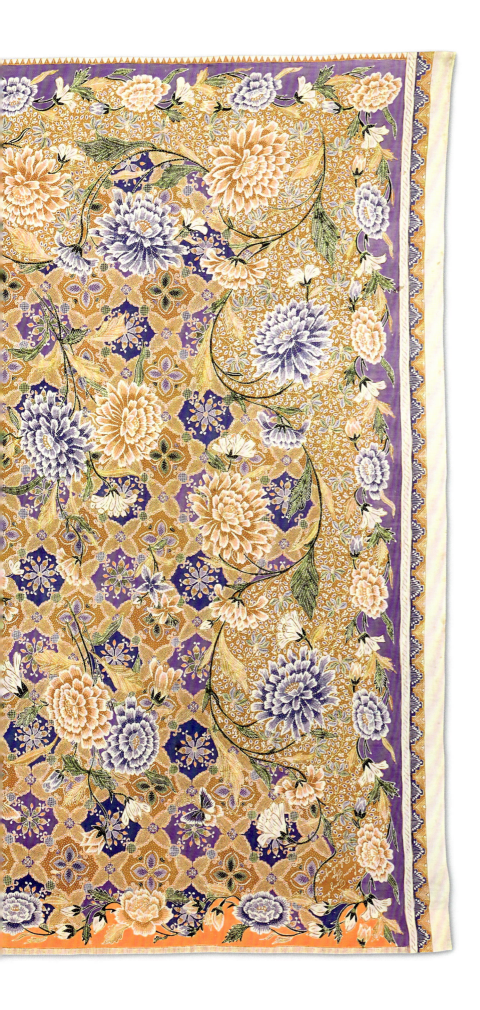

岢迪花卉纹裙布

20世纪40—60年代
长265.8厘米，宽110.3厘米
新加坡亚洲文明博物馆 藏

Batik Skirt Fabric with Flower
Motif
1940s—1960s
Length 265.8 cm, width 110.3 cm
Asian Civilisations Museum, Singapore

197

约1910年

两袖通长137.7厘米，衣长80厘米

新加坡土生文化馆 藏

Lee Kip Lee夫妇 赠

———

Kebaya

Approximately 1910

Full-length straight sleeves 137.7 cm, total length (back neck
to hem) 80 cm

20世纪30年代

两袖通长127.6厘米，衣长85.3厘米

新加坡土生文化馆 藏

Lee Kip Lee夫妇 赠

———————

Kebaya

1930s

Full-length straight sleeves 127.6 cm, total

length (back neck to hem) 85.3 cm

Peranakan Museum, Singapore

Gift of Mr and Mrs Lee Kip Lee

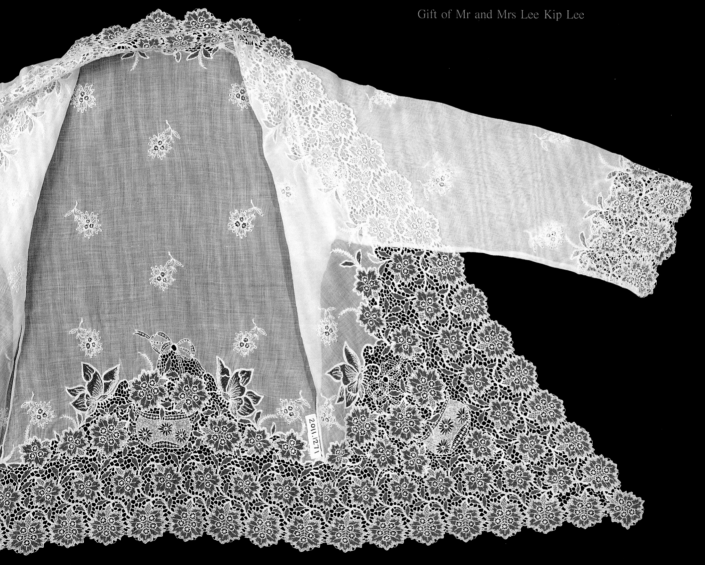

绣花可峇雅

20世纪30—60年代

两袖通长130厘米，衣长78厘米

新加坡亚洲文明博物馆 藏

2007年Anne Soh Gwek Shin女士为纪念Koh Suat Neo夫人所赠

Embroidered Kebaya

1930s—1960s

Full-length straight sleeves 130 cm, total length (back neck to hem) 78 cm

Asian Civilisations Museum, Singapore

Gift of Ms Anne Soh Gwek Shin in memory of Mdm Koh Suat Neo in 2007

彩绘孔雀纹纱笼

19世纪末至20世纪初

长88.8厘米，宽104.6厘米

新加坡土生文化馆 藏

Robbie Wowor 神父为纪念其祖母 Tan Tjien
Sian née Tjoa Soan Tjoe Nio 女士所赠。印度
尼西亚万鸦老

Painted Peacock Motif Sarong

Late 19th to early 20th century

Length 88.8 cm, width 104.6 cm

Peranakan Museum, Singapore

Gift of Father Robbie Wowor in memory of
grandmother, Mrs Tan Tjien Sian née Tjoa
Soan Tjoe Nio. Manado, Indonesia

彩绘花鸟纹纱笼

1919年

长192厘米，宽106厘米

新加坡土生文化馆 藏

Painted Flower and Bird Motifs Sarong

1919

Length 192 cm, width 106 cm

Peranakan Museum, Singapore

彩绘花鸟纹纱笼

19世纪末至20世纪初

长208.2厘米，宽105厘米

新加坡土生文化馆 藏

Robbie Wowor神父为纪念其祖母 Tan Tjien Sian née
Tjoa Soan Tjoe Nio 女士所赠。印度尼西亚万鸦老

Painted Flower and Bird Motifs Sarong

Late 19th to early 20th century

Length 208.2 cm, width 105 cm

Peranakan Museum, Singapore

Gift of Father Robbie Wowor in memory of
grandmother, Mrs Tan Tjien Sian née Tjoa Soan
Tjoe Nio. Manado, Indonesia

二

极为考究的娘惹配饰

娘惹身着传统服装时，对配饰的要求也极为考究，丰富多彩的娘惹配饰能够为娘惹服锦上添花。每到重大节日、生日、婚礼等重要时刻，娘惹们就会穿着鲜艳的薄纱可峇雅、纱笼和珠绣鞋，并佩戴华丽的首饰，盛装出席。娘惹装的配饰不仅作为装饰之用，还有更为深厚的文化历史意义，是一个娘惹家庭经济实力和社会地位的体现。

Exquisite Nyonya Accessories

Accessories are of particular importance to a Nyonya when dressed in traditional attire, with meticulous attention paid to their selection. The myriad of vibrant Nyonya accessories not only complements but also enhances the beauty of Nyonya attire. During significant occasions such as holidays, birthdays, weddings, and other momentous events, Nyonyas adorn themselves in colorful gauze Kebayas, Sarongs, bead-embroidered shoes, and lavish jewelry, meticulously attired to partake in the festivity.

Nyonya embellishments not only serve as decorations but also bear profound cultural and historical depth and connotations, symbolizing the economic and social status of a Nyonya family.

（一）彰显幸福的珠绣鞋

Bead-Embroidered Shoes: Symbolizing Happiness

珠绣鞋是娘惹服饰文化中重要组成部分，制作珠绣鞋是娘惹们必备的女红技能之一。成套的珠绣鞋是娘惹们不可或缺的嫁妆，她从小就学习"珠绣"技艺。出嫁时，娘惹会为自己未来的丈夫和公婆精心缝制珠绣鞋，婆家会将其他的珠绣品和珠绣鞋一起放在新房里，展示给亲朋好友看，以此来炫耀新娘的贤惠能干。

Bead-embroidered shoes are an integral part of Nyonya apparel culture. Crafting bead-embroidered shoes is considered an indispensable needlework skill and a virtuous tradition for Nyonya women. Sets of bead-embroidered shoes serve as vital components of a Nyonya woman's dowry. From a young age, she is initiated into the art of "bead-embroidery". Upon marriage, a Nyonya woman meticulously crafts bead-embroidered footwear for her future husband and in-laws. These pieces, alongside other bead-embroidered crafts, are proudly displayed in the newlyweds' room by the in-laws for guests, serving as a testament to the bride's virtues and adeptness.

花卉纹船型珠绣鞋

19世纪末至20世纪初
长23.7厘米，宽7.8厘米，高4.7厘米
新加坡土生文化馆 藏
Kok Putt Poh先生 赠

Boat-Shaped Beaded Shoes with Flower Motif
Late 19th to early 20th century
Length 23.7cm, width 7.8 cm, height 4.7 cm
Peranakan Museum, Singapore
Gift of Mr Kok Putt Poh

（二）突显财富和地位的珠宝首饰

Jewelry: Manifesting Wealth and Status

娘惹珠宝首饰的设计和制作也是丰富多元的娘惹文化的反映。珠宝首饰是娘惹家族社会地位与财富的标志。在其他文化中，珠宝通常是新娘嫁妆的一部分。娘惹通常有量身定做的珠宝首饰和饰品，因此许多首饰在形制或功能上的设计都自成一体，风格独特。20 世纪早期，家境殷实的娘惹至少拥有一套胸针配饰，这是正式场合必不可少的配饰，通常由黄金制作并且镶有钻石。

娘惹首饰的许多图案和元素都是借鉴、参照或修改自其他当地社区。斯里兰卡、印度、马来群岛和中国等地的工匠促进了土生珠宝的制作。

婚礼等喜庆场合的珠宝主要由黄金、钻石或其他半宝石制成。哀悼期则使用银、绿色或蓝色宝石和珍珠；珍珠被认为代表眼泪。许多妇女和儿童佩戴护身符（tangkal），以驱除邪恶、疾病和危险。

The design and production of Nyonya jewelry mirror the multifaceted culture of the Nyonyas. Jewelry serves as a benchmark of a Nyonya family's social stature and wealth. As in other cultures, it is often part of a bride's dowry. Nyonya women often possess custom-made jewelry, ensuring that each piece boasts a unique design, whether in shape, function, or intricate craftsmanship, showcasing the distinctive heritage of Nyonya style. In the early 20th century, affluent Nyonyas would at least own a set of brooches, an essential accessory for formal occasions, typically crafted from gold and embellished with diamonds. Many motifs and elements are borrowed, shared, or adapted from other local communities. Sri Lankan, Indian, Malay Archipelago, and Chinese artisans, among others, fuelled the creation of Peranakan jewellery.

Jewellery for celebratory occasions such as weddings was primarily made of gold and diamonds, or other semi-precious stones. During mourning periods, silver, green or blue coloured stones, and pearls were used; pearls were thought to represent tears. Many women and children wore protective amulets (tangkal) to ward off evil, illness, and danger.

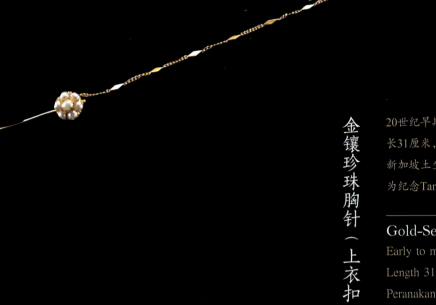

金镶珍珠胸针（上衣扣）

20世纪早期至中期
长31厘米，宽1.1厘米，高1厘米
新加坡土生文化馆 藏
为纪念Tan Tjien Sian Manado家族而赠

Gold-Set Pearl Kerosang (Blouse Fasteners)

Early to mid-20th century
Length 31 cm, width 1.1 cm, height 1 cm
Peranakan Museum, Singapore
Gift in memory of family Tan Tjien Sian Manado

金胸针（上衣扣）

20世纪早期至中期
长28.5厘米，宽1.2厘米
新加坡亚洲文明博物馆 藏
Edmond Chin先生 赠

Gold Kerosang (Blouse Fasteners)

Early to mid-20th century
Length 28.5 cm, width 1.2 cm
Asian Civilisations Museum, Singapore
Gift of Mr Edmond Chin

金胸针（上衣扣）

20世纪早期至中期
长18.5厘米
新加坡亚洲文明博物馆 藏

Gold Kerosang (Blouse Fasteners)

Early to mid-20th century
Length 18.5 cm
Asian Civilisations Museum, Singapore

金质皮带扣

19世纪末至20世纪初

长10厘米，宽7.5厘米

新加坡亚洲文明博物馆 藏

Edmond Chin先生 赠

—————————

Gold Belt Buckle

Late 19th to early 20th century

Length 10 cm, width 7.5 cm

Asian Civilisations Museum, Singapore

Gift of Mr Edmond Chin

金质椭圆形皮带扣

19世纪末至20世纪初

长15.5厘米，宽11.5厘米

新加坡亚洲文明博物馆 藏

—————————

Gold Oval Belt Buckle

Late 19th to early 20th century

Length 15.5 cm, width 11.5 cm

Asian Civilisations Museum, Singapore

金
镶
钻
花
形
胸
针
（
上
衣
扣
）

20世纪早期至中期

A：长3.7厘米，宽1.3厘米，高5厘米

B：长3.7厘米，宽1.3厘米，高5.2厘米

C：长3.7厘米，宽1.3厘米，高5.2厘米

新加坡亚洲文明博物馆 藏

Edmond Chin先生 赠

Gold-Set Diamond Floral Kerosang (Blouse Fasteners)

Early to mid-20th century

A: Length 3.7 cm, width 1.3 cm, height 5 cm

B: Length 3.7 cm, width 1.3 cm, height 5.2 cm

C: Length 3.7 cm, width 1.3 cm, height 5.2 cm

Asian Civilisations Museum, Singapore

Gift of Mr Edmond Chin

金胸针（上衣扣）

20世纪早期至中期

长29厘米，宽0.8厘米，高4.8厘米

新加坡亚洲文明博物馆 藏

Edmond Chin先生 赠

Gold Kerosang (Blouse Fasteners)

Early to mid-20th century

Length 29 cm, width 0.8 cm, height 4.8 cm

Asian Civilisations Museum, Singapore

Gift of Mr Edmond Chin

20世纪早期至中期

长28.3厘米，宽0.6厘米，高1.1厘米

新加坡土生文化馆 藏

金镶钻花形胸针（上衣扣）

Gold-Set Diamond Floral Kerosang (Blouse Fasteners)

Early to mid-20th century

Length 28.3 cm, width 0.6 cm, height 1.1 cm

Peranakan Museum, Singapore

金
镶
钻
花
形
胸
针
（
上
衣
扣
）

19世纪末至20世纪初

长6.9厘米，高4.5厘米

新加坡亚洲文明博物馆　藏

Edmond Chin先生　赠

Gold-Set Diamond Floral Brooch Kerosang (Blouse Fasteners)

Late 19th to early 20th century

Length 6.9 cm, height 4.5 cm

Asian Civilisations Museum, Singapore

Gift of Mr Edmond Chin

金质动物纹腰带

19世纪末至20世纪初

长80.5厘米

新加坡亚洲文明博物馆 藏

Edmond Chin先生赠

Gold Belt with Animal Motif

Late 19th to early 20th century

Length 80.5 cm

Collection of the Asian Civilisations Museum, Singapore

Gift of Mr Edmond Chin

这条精致的腰带有一个腰带扣和19块面板，每一块都有一个动物图案，主要在庆祝场合佩戴。

This exquisite belt consists of a belt buckle and 19 panels, each adorned with an animal motif. It was typically worn on ceremonial occasions.

223

银
质
钱
包

19世纪末至20世纪初
长13.1厘米，宽26.7厘米
新加坡国家博物馆 藏
Xu Cheng Bin先生 赠

Silver Purse
Late 19th to early 20th century
Length 13.1 cm, width 26.7 cm
National Museum of Singapore
Gift of Mr Xu Cheng Bin

銀鍍金發簪

19世纪末至20世纪初

A：长12厘米，宽2.7厘米，高2.4厘米

B：长15厘米，宽2.8厘米，高2.5厘米

新加坡亚洲文明博物馆 藏

Edmond Chin先生 赠

Gold-Plated Silver Hairpin

Late 19th to early 20th century

A: Length 12 cm, width 2.7 cm, height 2.4 cm

B: Length 15 cm, width 2.8 cm, height 2.5 cm

Asian Civilisations Museum, Singapore

Gift of Mr Edmond Chin

传统娘惹们会将长发盘起，并用簪子来固定。

Traditional Peranakan women would coil their long hair and secure it with hairpins like these.

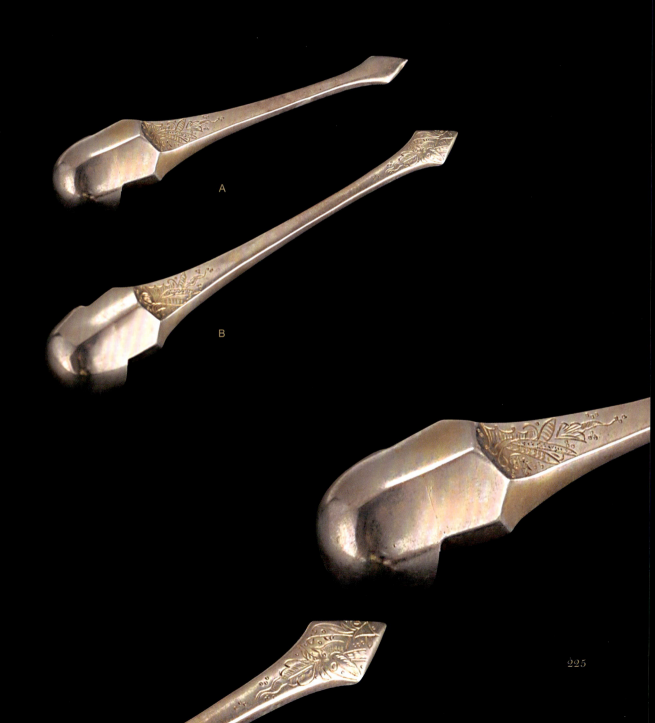

三 传统与现代的娘惹文化

传统文化参与当代艺术设计，融入现代文化潮流已成为当今的风尚。娘惹文化历经传统与当代的多重碰撞与对接，使民族的与时尚的元素产生融合，继而使其鲜明、主动又开放的文化魅力得以大放异彩。

Nyonya Culture: From Tradition to Modernity

The active engagement of traditional culture in contemporary art design and its seamless integration into the currents of modern culture have become today's trend. Nyonya culture has undergone a series of harmonious encounters and connections between the traditional and the contemporary, fostering a synergistic fusion of ethnic authenticity with contemporary flair. This process has unveiled the unique and dynamic charm of Nyonya culture, allowing its vivid, proactive, and inclusive cultural allure to thrive.

娘惹服饰的当代表现
Contemporary Expression of Nyonya Attire

服饰是一个民族特质最直观的体现。从宽松过长的长衫到修身精美的可峇雅，从朴素深沉的单色调到对比强烈的多种色彩，从简单的几何纹饰到夸张多样的立体图案，娘惹服饰一直随着时代在变化。

Attire stands as a vivid reflection of a nation's characteristics. Spanning from the elegantly loose and elongated baju panjang to the exquisitely tailored Kebayas, from the depth of monochrome to the vibrancy of contrasting colors, and from the simplicity of geometric patterns to the bold diversity of three-dimensional designs, Nyonya attire has continuously evolved over time.

结语 **Conclusion**

　　"文明因交流而多彩，文明因互鉴而丰富。"在峇峇娘惹的历史发展中，他们既传承了中国文化的精髓，同时也与东南亚定居地的社区紧密交融，共同孕育出了一个充满活力的融合文化。这一持续的文化融合与演化，不仅彰显了华人文化的包容性与创造力，也体现了东南亚社区对他们的接纳与融合的开放态度。

　　今日所称的"土生社区"泛指一系列具有融合遗产的社群，除了峇峇娘惹（即土生华人）之外，还包括马六甲的仄迪人（或称土生印度人）、爪哇土生人以及土生阿拉伯人。他们共同的特点在于，各自独特的祖先文化——无论是来自中国、印度、阿拉伯还是欧洲——都与马来群岛的本土文化相融合。

　　土生文化的诸多方面如今已成为新加坡、马来西亚和印度尼西亚热议的话题。土生社区的手工艺品、时装和美食文化愈发受到人们的喜爱，部分人士甚至尝试复兴诸如讲峇峇马来语之类的文化实践活动。尽管这些传统习俗在过去几个世纪可能经历了变迁，但许多峇峇娘惹仍深深地认同并自豪于他们多元文化遗产的丰富多样性和包容性。

　　峇峇娘惹文化不断地为其在东南亚定居的社会作出贡献，恰恰印证了"文明交流互鉴，是推动人类文明进步和世界和平发展的重要动力"。

"Civilizations have become richer and more colorful with exchanges and mutual learning."

In the course of their history, the Baba Nyonya have not only inherited Chinese culture but have also closely interacted and assimilated with the Southeast Asian communities they settled in, forming a vibrant hybrid culture. The continuous integration and evolution of their culture demonstrates not only the Chinese culture's capacity for inclusiveness and innovation but also of the Southeast Asian communities that received them.

"Peranakan" today refers to a range of mixed heritage communities. Their unifying trait is the blending of ancestral cultures—Chinese, Indian, Arab, European, and others—with the indigenous cultures of the Malay Archipelago. Besides Baba Nyonya, there are the Chitty Melakans or Peranakan Indians, Jawi Peranakans, and Arab Peranakans.

Aspects of Peranakan culture are now the focus of debate and revival across Singapore, Malaysia, and Indonesia. Peranakan crafts, fashion, and cuisine are increasingly popular, and some have sought to revive cultural practices such as speaking Baba Malay. These customs and practices may have changed over the centuries, but a keen sense of identity and pride in the diversity and inclusiveness of their multicultural heritage remains among many Baba Nyonya.

The continuing contributions of the Baba Nyonya to the development of the Southeast Asian societies they settled in emphatically illustrate that "exchanges and mutual learning among civilizations are pivotal in driving the advancement of human civilization and fostering the development of global peace."

"峇峇娘惹的世界——海上丝绸之路上的峇峇娘惹文化展"策展解析

李其仁

中国（海南）南海博物馆

经过3年多的酝酿，2024年3月—7月，中国（海南）南海博物馆与中国文物保护基金会合作举办"峇峇娘惹的世界——海上丝绸之路上的峇峇娘惹文化展"（以下简称"峇峇娘惹文化展"）。通过展出新加坡亚洲文明博物馆和新加坡土生文化馆借展的124件（套）文物及中国（海南）南海博物馆11件（套）馆藏土生华人家具，向观众多角度展示峇峇娘惹世界中的重要文化元素，深化观众对土生华人文化的认识。为相关研究者提供丰富的实证材料，深化对古代海上贸易、文化交流模式以及海上丝绸之路沿线国家和地区历史发展的理解。本文将浅析"峇峇娘惹文化展"筹备过程中的策展视角、创意构思、资源整合等方面的内容，不足之处，请专家、同行批评指正。

一、策展视角：海上丝绸之路与多元文化融合

东南亚地区是海上丝绸之路途经的重要区域，也是多元文化融合发展的聚集地。其文化有本土文化衍生出来的，也有一大部分是由外来社群和当地社群在交融中形成的。早在15世纪，在马来半岛、爪哇岛北部海岸、苏门答腊岛甚至印度尼西亚东部群岛沿岸，就有一些华人移民的混合社区，他们大部分人的原籍是福建或广东潮汕地区。"中国商船均云集港内，每年初春顺西北季候风南来，夏季则顺东南季候风而返。其时，马六甲华侨大都来自闽省，男女顶结髻，习俗同中国，全城房屋，悉仿中国式，俨然为海外中国的城市"[1]。这些早期的东南亚中国移民几乎都是男性，他们与当地非华人女性通婚的现象非常普遍。峇峇（Baba）娘惹（Nyonya），或称土生华人（Peranakan Chinese），就是这群15世纪初定居在东南亚一带的中国移民和当地土著通婚后所生的后代，主要集中在新加坡，马来西亚的马六甲、槟城和印度尼西亚的雅加达。

---

[1] 宋哲美：《马来西亚华人史》，中华文化事业公司，1964年，第51页。

对于峇峇娘惹这个社群，大部分的中国观众是陌生的。那么在这样一个陌生的主题下，展览如何做出亮点，如何做出一个观众看得懂、有共鸣的展览？经过策展团队多次的沟通、交流，决定从"海上丝绸之路"和"多元文化融合"的视角展开。

中国（海南）南海博物馆自2018年开馆以来，立足自身定位，策划实施了"龙行万里——海上丝绸之路上的龙泉青瓷""绿色黄金——海上丝绸之路上的茶叶贸易""诗画彩瓷——唐代海上丝绸之路上的长沙窑瓷器展""海药本草——唐宋时期海上丝绸之路上的香药"等主题的海上丝绸之路系列展览，致力于将本馆打造成"21世纪海上丝绸之路"文化交流的重要平台。峇峇娘惹的先辈们沿着海上丝绸之路前往东南亚地区开展贸易，之后定居东南亚，因此以"海上丝绸之路"作为策展视角是非常符合主题的。

峇峇娘惹虽地处东南亚地区，却继承了许多中国传统文化中的内容，特别是在文化习俗和宗教信仰等方面有明显的中华元素。同时，马来人等土著的语言、服饰和饮食习惯也融进了土生华人的日常生活，马六甲大型港口城市的国际化特征和土生华人以贸易为生的特点，也使得欧洲等世界其他地区的文化元素，一同对土生华人社群进行着塑造。土生华人的文化根源是中华文化，但在其发展过程中同样受到了东南亚本土文化和欧洲文化的影响。因此，无论是语言、宗教信仰、文化习俗，还是身份认同，都形成了自有的独特文化，也展现了中华文化的持久影响力。因此，策展团队决定以"多元文化融合"贯穿整个展览。

二、内容设计

对于这个陌生的选题，策展团队希望通过来自新加坡文博单位124件（套）藏品，向中国观众讲述峇峇娘惹的奋斗史，以及他们所从事的贸易活动、追求的多种信仰和创造的物质、非物质文化遗产等内容。通过展览，展示他们自强不息的奋斗精神、包容进取的广阔胸怀，以及跨越文化壁垒实现融合创新的在地文化。展览叙事并不限于时间上的线性阐释，而是从五个不同层面讲述一个移民社群是如何通过跨文化融合来创造独特文化的有趣故事，以体现当今多元文化世界中的开放与包容，同时也是华人文化包容性和创新性的体现。

展览内容以土生华人收藏的体现各种物质、非物质文化元素的展品为中心，将这些展品按照使用价值和内在价值的区别分为五个单元："创造历史的一代先驱""海上贸易推动的文化融合""多元文化融合的信仰""中西结合的婚俗文化""传统与现代的娘惹时尚"。平行的内容架构，没有追求严格的内容逻辑顺序，这使展览可以一种更加开放、自由流动的方式呈现，从而使每个主题都能被独立体现。

第一单元"创造历史的一代先驱"，借助时间线介绍峇峇娘惹社区的形成和发展，以及土生华人领袖为华人社群所做的贡献。在这部分，我们重点展示陈明远（Tan Beng Wan）夫妇肖像画（复制）、一套土生华人家具和槟榔盒套装（图1）。

陈明远夫妇是一对土生华人，他们的服饰融合了中国和东南亚元素，是早期土生华人文化的标志。肖像画中陈明远先生身着中国传统服装，这是当时土生华人男性的标准搭配，同时旁边还放置一套《东周列国》（图2）。

陈明远夫人身着长衫，胸前以三枚胸针固定，长衫罩着里面的裙布，是当时东南亚女性的常规穿着。她旁边放着一套槟榔盒用具及一个瓷痰盂。土生华人嚼的是生槟榔，即将槟榔叶、槟榔果、石灰，搭配棕

图1　陈明远夫妇肖像画（复制）实景图　　　　　　　　　　　图2　方几中的《东周列国》

儿茶、丁香或烟草放入嘴里咀嚼，其后将咀嚼出的红色汁液吐在痰盂中，这与海南当地民众吃生槟榔的方式相似。

　　第二单元"海上贸易推动的文化融合"，介绍因海上贸易带来的文化交融。土生华人家庭中的厨房器皿、日常用品和礼仪用品，比如各类瓷器，是土生华人在中国定制的，这些瓷器在设计上适用于土生华人的审美和生活方式，而其他多元文化元素融合的日常用品则体现了土生华人独特的文化特点，这部分重点展示在一批娘惹瓷与中国（海南）南海博物馆馆藏土生华人家具中。

　　"娘惹瓷（Nyonya Ware），主要是指晚清民国时期（19世纪中期至20世纪二三十年代）东南亚马六甲海峡一带（主要是马六甲、槟榔屿、新加坡三地）的土生华人从景德镇专门订制的一种粉彩瓷器，常饰凤凰牡丹图案，用于喜庆场合如婚礼，寿宴，春节等，后来也用于日常生活。"[1]娘惹瓷器色泽鲜亮、对比强烈、设计精美，饰有象征意味的中国传统纹样，纹饰及颜色各具特色。娘惹瓷常用中国传统的凤凰牡丹纹，且有一个或多个开光。颜色一般使用白、绿、粉、红、黄等过渡色（图3）。

　　第三单元"多元文化融合的信仰"，多元文化的融合与影响，使得峇峇娘惹社区所奉行的信仰也呈现出多元性的特点。本单元以土生华人的传统家神供桌为重点，结合供品和瓷器做装饰，体现出神灵供奉、祖先崇拜是土生华人传统文化的一个重要特征。同时，受到西方文化的影响，有一些土生华人选择了信奉基督教等外来宗教。

　　第四单元"中西结合的婚俗文化"，本单元介绍土生华人源于中国的传统婚礼及繁复隆重的婚礼仪式。我们以土生华人婚俗中最为代表性的两张婚床为重点，向观众展示婚礼期间的婚床装饰和婚礼用品。峇峇娘惹的婚俗文化保留了大量华人的传统习俗，峇峇娘惹的婚礼也是东南亚颇有特色的婚礼之一。峇峇娘惹们接触着西方文化，也受到马来文化潜移默化的影响，又保留着古老的华人传统和习惯，这使得他们在婚俗仪礼的传承中兼容发展、多元融合。

---

[1] 熊寰：《娘惹瓷》，《中国陶瓷工业》2006年第2期。

图3　娘惹瓷

第五单元"传统与现代的娘惹时尚"，峇峇娘惹文化是多元文化交流互融结果的反映，它既是混合的，也是创新的，为重新定位和思考亚洲的传统时尚提出了新的概念。本单元以娘惹的服装和珠宝首饰为亮点，介绍"峇峇娘惹"中极具特色的娘惹服饰，将明艳独特的着装和风格各异的珠宝首饰组合在一起，可以立体地展现娘惹文化中的美学与时尚。娘惹服饰在款式、颜色、纹饰等方面融合了中国传统文化、马来文化及西方文化的因素，是峇峇娘惹社群适应在地生活的典型代表之一。

三、形式设计

"围绕主题、突出特色、提炼元素、烘托氛围是临时展览形式设计的重要内容。重点文物、色彩基调以及具有意义的图案图腾、时代背景所产生的艺术联想等都是临时展览特有的艺术符号。将艺术符号提炼为艺术元素，并对艺术元素加以利用，有助于营造展览氛围，使设计呈现饱满的效果。"[1] 在整体形式设计中，策展团队就展览设计风格、流线、颜色选择、场景搭建等内容开展多次讨论，以确保形式设计在做到对展览主题及内容的准确表达外，还能让展览效果更加出彩。为了让观众更好融入展览，身临其境感受峇峇娘惹文化的魅力。序厅部分，设计团队设计搭建了峇峇娘惹祖屋中独特的排屋内庭装饰（图4），营造峇峇娘惹世界的氛围感及拉近观众与峇峇娘惹的距离感。同时在序厅部分，设计团队设计了一个大型展标，其中运用了峇峇娘惹常用的白、绿、粉、红、黄五种颜色元素进行组合，不仅给观众带来视觉冲击，同时也对展览主题有了一个非常好的诠释作用，设计效果非常出彩。此外，设计团队复原了峇峇娘惹婚礼期间的婚床场景（图5）及客厅场景（图6），丰富展厅空间感，营造出一个沉浸式体验空间。

颜色的运用是此次展览的重点。峇峇娘惹文化中，常用白、绿、粉、红、黄等过渡色，这些颜色饱和度低，在设计过程中极难把握，策展团队就颜色问题多次讨论，经过反复调色、对比、打样，才最终将颜色确定出来。无论是展厅整体氛围营造（图7），还是具体的展标、单元版、海报设计（图8）等，均离不开颜色。

[1] 张乐：《南京博物院临时展览形式设计案例分析》，《东南文化》2023年第1期。

图4　序厅场景

图5　婚床场景

图6　家具场景

图7　展厅一角

图8　宣传海报

四、展览延伸

社教活动和文创开发不仅是展览内容的延伸和补充，而且能将展览以另一种形式呈现给观众，真正让展览走进生活。自开展以来，我馆开展了767场展览讲解活动，组织策划16场"娘惹服饰风尚秀""娘惹的珠绣""娘惹的厨房""娘惹的衣橱""峇峇娘惹&琼海溜的茶话会"等主题社教活动，观众积极踊跃报名、参与度高。

文创设计持续发力，围绕展览主题、文物元素提取，设计开发出110款文创产品（图9），销售近25000件，让观众把展览带回家。

良好的展出效果，除展览本身外，也离不开宣传团队。展览期间，人民网、《中国日报》等媒体发文总量598条，互动声量703.92万，影响力值3.15亿。

图9 文创产品

五、结语

"峇峇娘惹文化展"以多元文化融合为策展理念,通过为期4个月的展出及配套的讲解、主题社教活动和文创产品,在中国(海南)南海博物馆掀起一股"南洋风"。对于入境展,由于双方的策展习惯、展出方式有一定的区别,因此需要加强沟通,熟悉展览的信息,才能更好地在原展览的基础之上,结合自身办展理念,进一步深化展览内容。同时需在展览大纲、形式设计上做出自身特色,切勿照抄照搬。

峇峇娘惹建筑室内屏门的装饰艺术初探

吴伟义

中国（海南）南海博物馆

峇峇娘惹是15世纪初期定居在马六甲、印尼、新加坡等一带的华人与当地人通婚后形成的特殊族群[1]。他们既保留了部分中华传统文化，又融合了大量当地文化与西方文化，形成独特的峇峇娘惹文化。其居所建筑风格也独具特色，融合了中式的木雕、石雕等工艺与马来建筑的空间布局以及西方建筑的装饰手法等，形成一种既精致又有地域风情的建筑风格。

峇峇娘惹建筑（以下简称娘惹建筑）保留部分中国古建筑特色的布局，并且大量使用具有中国文化寓意的装饰，这表明他们在建筑上传承了中国传统文化的元素，即使在与当地文化和西方文化融合的过程中，仍然重视和保留了自己的文化根源。屏门作为娘惹建筑中最具有视觉特色之一的建筑构件，承担中华文化在海外输出的重要符号，本文聚焦这一"符号"以马来西亚槟城侨生博物馆（Pinang Peranakan Mansion）中前厅与天井之间的屏门（图1）为主视角，通过装饰的题材、工艺、内涵等方面，分析屏门上一系列具有中国传统文化特色的纹饰。

一、娘惹建筑的文化信息

娘惹建筑是充分体现娘惹文化的重要载体，它采取中西结合的风格，较为典型地反映了中国建筑文化在南洋的传播和融合。其布局上深受中国古建筑风格影响，保留了中国闽南地区、潮汕地区的建筑特色，院落内部空间以"进"为纵向排列单位，与闽南古厝的"一条龙式"相似，为一字排开[2]。屋内较为宽阔敞亮，喜好摆放木质雕花家具，一般设有天井，便于采光、通风。从建筑布局和装饰元素可以看出峇峇娘惹建筑在文化碰撞交流中对中华文化的传承与坚持。

[1] 张燕：《东南亚裔美国小说研究》，暨南大学出版社，2022年，第180页。
[2] 余玉：《浅谈中马文化融合的图景——以娘惹文化为例》，《青年文学家》2020年第36期。

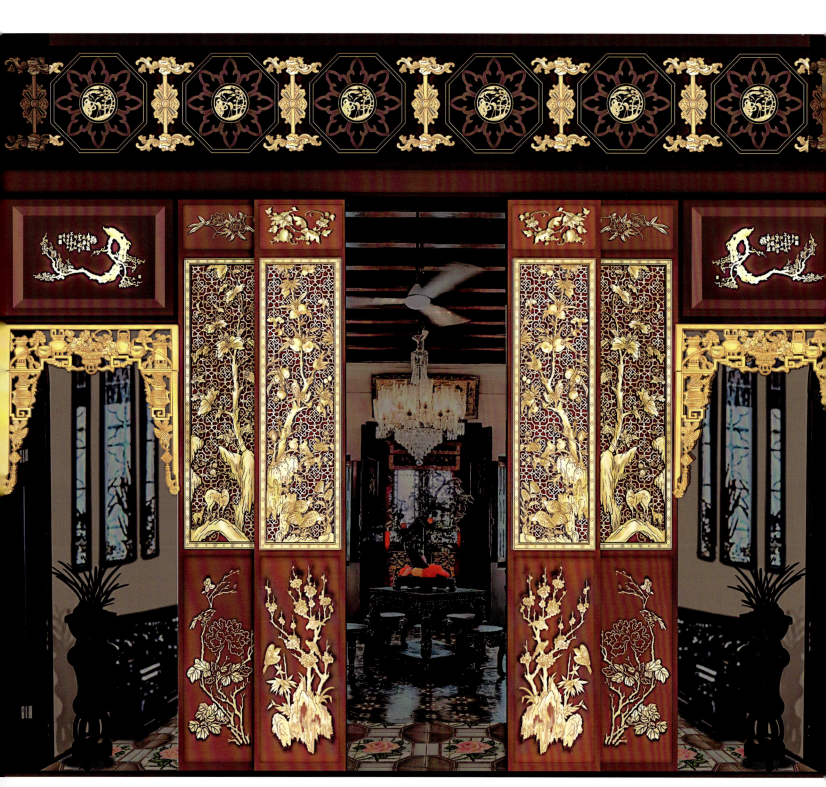

图1　前厅与天井之间的屏门背面全貌（笔者自绘）

二、娘惹建筑中的屏门及其结构

屏门是整个隔门面用木板钉起、表面光洁的一种门型，因作用类似屏风而得名[1]。屏门在南北方的具体造法与含义多有不同，在北方多用于四合院垂花门后檐柱间，半壁游廊柱间或作为院墙侧门等，而在闽南、潮汕一带，人们将庭院厅堂与天井之间的隔断门叫作进屏门。这种建筑装饰在潮汕民居中很常见，"四点金"以上规模的民居门楼内都设有进屏门[2]。这类屏门的门扇数目为偶数，并根据实际的空间距离确定。由此可见，娘惹建筑中的屏门与此类可谓一脉相承。作为娘惹建筑特色元素之一，屏门在娘惹建筑的"进深式"的空间布局中起到关键作用，首先，从视觉美学的角度看，屏门在室内空间占有较大的面积，是空间的主视觉，其美感在追求"中式巴洛克"风格的空间设计之初就已定调，必须有富贵华丽且寓意美好的纹饰进行填充。其次，屏门作为前后空间的"隔断"，除空间上满足物理阻隔功能外，保证内部空间的活动隐私与视觉秩序。如果单从中国传统建筑文化解读，其隔绝外部气场的作用还蕴藏一定民间风水学内涵。

娘惹建筑中的屏门设置，在中国传统建筑中可以算是太师壁[3]中的一种，其空间位置与功能是室内隔断，结构上也具有一定的自身特色，在构件主体两旁靠墙处都有小门可以出入，只不过太师壁中间的壁面虽有若干扇槅扇组合而成，或用棂条拼成各种花纹，也有做板壁，但一般不作为进出口，因此一般会在壁前放置条几案等家具及各种陈设，而娘惹建筑中的屏门是可以具体作为出入口。我们以马来西亚槟城侨生博物馆（Pinang Peranakan Mansion，以下简称娘惹博物馆）中正门前厅（会客厅）通往天井之间的进屏门为例，其主要结构如图2所示。图中槛框起到整体排布划分与固定的作用，左右两侧门就以槛框圈定，其上面各有装饰罩；中间主体为隔扇门，设置偶数的门扇数，一般为四到八扇，这里设置六扇；隔扇门一般又分为上下束腰、槅心、裙板三个主要部分，不过这里只有上束腰，且镶有绦环板。

三、娘惹建筑中屏门的装饰题材与含义

娘惹建筑中屏门的装饰一般是双面雕刻装饰图样，具有较高的艺术价值，双面的美化，可供进屏门内外双方都可以欣赏[4]。本章节将用于屏门上的装饰题材（分布见图2）与含义分四部分进行分类讨论，第一部分以"福""禄""寿"作为该类吉祥装饰题材的基调，第二、第三部分按照装饰物象的自然属性和艺术化的角度将纹饰分为动、植物两大类，试图归纳和理解娘惹建筑中沿用中国传统建筑木雕或者说中国传统吉祥纹样的用意，第四部分介绍相关的文字类装饰。除此之外，还会对一些在此建筑或其他地区娘惹建筑中具有代表性纹饰的屏门构件加以讨论。

[1] 王俊：《中国古代门窗》，中国商业出版社，2022年，第58页。
[2] 王春法主编：《雕绘乾坤——潮州木雕展》，北京时代华文书局，2020年，第164页。
[3]（加）王其钧：《中国建筑图解词典》，机械工业出版社，2021年，第224页。
[4] 王春法主编：《雕绘乾坤——潮州木雕展》，北京时代华文书局，2020年，第164页。

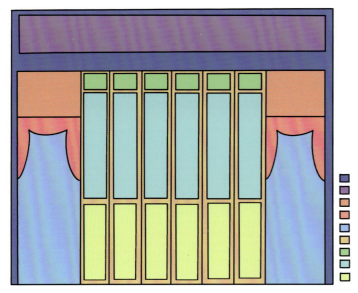

色标	结构名称	纹饰	
		正面	背面
■	槛框	楹联	无
■	横批窗	卷草、瓶花、丝瓜、梧桐、仙鹤	
■	帘架心（横批）	麟凤图	梅花
■	飞罩	博古清供、瑞兽合福	
■	左右通道口	无	
■	槅扇门框（边抹）	无	
■	绦环板	瓜瓞延绵图	秋葵图
■	槅心	对鸡、鸳鸯、母子鹿、石榴、桂花、牡丹花	
■	裙板	寿石、竹、喜上眉梢	牡丹、白头翁

图2　屏门结构与纹饰分布图（笔者自制）

（一）"福""禄""寿"

中国传统建筑木构件纹饰蕴含着丰富的文化内涵，"福""禄""寿"是其中极具代表性的主题，"福""禄""寿"的主题纹饰在漫长的历史发展中，逐渐趋于稳定，形成中国传统文化中对美好生活的向往和祈愿。娘惹建筑将这一富有美好寓意的纹饰进行了融合传承。"福"在中国文化中是最可以体现人们美好期许的字样之一，有着幸福、福气、福运等美好寓意，涵盖了生活的各个方面，包括物质的富足、家庭的美满、身心的健康等。在建筑中，除了文字形式，还有一些与"福"相关的图案，如蝙蝠纹。蝙蝠的"蝠"与"福"同音，因此蝙蝠成为了"福"的象征。在进屏门两端的飞罩处雕有蝙蝠纹藏在器物中，介于器身与器盖之间，有"合福"之意。

"禄"通常指俸禄，代表着功名利禄、仕途顺利等含义。它反映了古代社会人们对社会地位和经济收入的追求，是一种对事业成功和社会认可的期望。在屏门的木构件上，"禄"纹饰常常以鹿纹的形式出现。因为"鹿"与"禄"同音，鹿纹的造型丰富多样。传统木雕一般表现一只矫健的雄鹿，昂首挺胸，展现出勃勃生机，而进屏门槅心雕刻的是母子鹿，寓意着家族的繁衍和传承与禄运的延续有关。另有一些与禄相关的植物纹饰，如灵芝纹。灵芝在古代被视为仙草，具有吉祥如意的寓意和延年益寿的功效，同时也与禄运相关联，象征着能够获得高官厚禄。

"寿"代表着长寿、健康、延年益寿的意思。它体现了人们对生命的珍视和对长寿的渴望，是中国传统文化中对生命质量和长度的念想。最常见的"寿"纹饰是寿字纹。寿字的写法有很多种，如圆形的团寿纹，线条流畅圆润，给人一种和谐美满的感觉。与"寿"相关的图案还有松鹤纹。松树四季常青，象征着长寿和坚韧；鹤被视为仙禽，具有长寿的象征意义。松鹤组合在一起，更加强化了长寿的寓意，不过在进屏门横批窗的团形纹饰较有特色，雕刻的是仙鹤与梧桐树的组合，寓意"天地同寿"。

（二）花卉植物

在中国传统吉祥纹样中，自然界众多的花卉植物都有其美好且特定的寓意，娘惹建筑中的木雕构件大量吸收和传承这一文化现象。第一类是折枝花卉或果实，这类装饰纹样是将其自然生长的状态艺术性地契合在进屏门的各个部件中，例如槛框雕板中镶有丝瓜；中间隔扇门的槅心处雕有荷花、石榴树、柿树、桂花树、鸡冠花；隔扇门的裙板装饰有牡丹花、梅花；隔扇门的顶部束腰装饰有秋葵、南瓜。上述这些纹饰紧紧围绕屋主对生活的美好祈愿，例如，丝瓜、石榴、南瓜、秋葵都有"多籽"对应"多子"，象征多子多福、子嗣绵延，值得注意的是，在南瓜边上还点缀一只展翅的蝴蝶，这类组合在中国传统吉祥纹样中称为"瓜瓞绵绵"，"蝶"与"瓞"同音，瓞为小瓜，寓子孙万代之意[1]。荷花、桂花、梅花都是被赋予培养品格，修身养性的含义，具有教育警示的寓意，柿树、鸡冠花、牡丹则是利事富贵的象征。我们会发现以上这一系列纹饰具有完善的内在逻辑，形成一个周而复始，代代相传的文化现象。

第二类为"清供"或者"博古"一类，如图3在隔扇门的左右侧门的花罩上主要以填装饱满花卉的编织篮和一些博古器具组成。"清供"主题纹饰历史悠久与插花艺术有着密切联系，是文人雅士之日常喜好的具体表现，明清时期多有文人描绘此类画作，画面中有瓜果、文具、瓶插花卉等。"博古"类是闽南、潮州一带善用的木雕装饰题材，图式中常有瓶、罐、壶、碗、盘、盒、盂等，这些器物通常被刻画得非常精细，还能够反映出主人的文化素养和审美情趣。

除上述两类之外，另有装饰性元素的花卉植物，主要用以辅助装饰作用，例如卷草纹，以及一些边框上大小一致排列均匀的小花朵。

（三）珍禽瑞兽

除了被赋予"福""禄""寿"特定含义的鹿、蝙蝠、仙鹤，还有许多象征祥瑞的动物出现在屏门的装饰中。第一类是有吉祥寓意的禽鸟，例如中间三对隔扇门的槅心左右内容成对，它们分别为公鸡、鸳鸯、喜鹊及其他小体鸟类，他们均成双成对出现在画面中，搭配前文提到的象征"多子多福""吉祥如意"的花卉果实，更多要补充传达夫妻和睦、家庭美满的含义。而其中公鸡（图4）的出现引人注目，公鸡被誉为"五德之禽"，鸡的"冠"与"官"相谐，具有文德之意。一对雄鸡立于鸡冠花之中，二者组合，"官"上加"官"，更有驱邪避害、以德化人、扬名立万的寓意。

---

[1] 李学英编：《中国传统吉祥图案精粹》，天津人民美术出版社，2006年。

图3 博古题材飞罩（笔者自绘）

图4 槅心上的"公鸡与鸡冠花"

第二类是瑞兽，除上文提到的"母子鹿"外，娘惹建筑的屏门上也不乏狻猊、麒麟等祥瑞神兽。"麟凤图"位于该进屏门左右两端小门正面的帘架横批处，凤凰与麒麟的组合早在汉代画像石中就有出现，是成型较早的吉祥图样，宋赵明诚《金石录》卷十四《汉麟凤赞并记》载："按《汉史》，安帝时，频有凤凰麒麟之瑞。"[1] "永建元年秋七月。山阳太守河内孙君新刻瑞像麟凤。"[2] 值得注意的是，在上述"清供"花飞罩两侧下落的末端各装饰有一只异兽（图5），十分特别，该异兽短头似龙首，带喙，鱼身有爪，且浑身布满鳞片，背部生有羽翼。查阅资料，从造型的角度分析，该异兽出处有两种可能，一是在中国南方古民居中常见的木雕构件"鳌鱼"，其形态与图6[3]中的描绘相类似，鳌鱼有"鱼化龙"的内涵，寓意子孙后代能够出人头地。二是在《山海经》中确有记载一类名为"文鳐鱼"的造型也符合这类异兽形象，原文中写道："又西百八十里，曰泰器之山。观水出焉，西流注于流沙。是多文鳐鱼，状如鲤鱼，鱼身而鸟翼，苍文而白首赤喙。常行西海，游于东海，以夜飞。其音如鸾鸡，其味酸甘，食之已狂，见则天下大穰。"[4] 从原文的描述，可以了解到文鳐鱼的好处至少有两种，第一是治愈癫狂之症，第二是见之者"大穰"即"大丰收"。总之二者皆有祥瑞之意。

[1]（宋）赵明诚：《金石录》影印本，中华书局，1980年。
[2]（宋）米芾撰，刘世军、黄三艳校注：《画史校注》，广西师范大学出版社，2020年，第179页。
[3] 陈永发绘著，云南省大理州城乡建设环境保护局编：《白族木雕图案》，云南美术出版社，1995年，第101页。
[4] 谷瑞丽、赵发国译注：《山海经》，崇文书局，2023年，第41页。

图5 异兽

图6 建筑木雕构件中的鳌鱼

（四）文辞装饰

直接的文字装饰在屏门上并不多，例如进屏门中间隔扇的左右楹框上挂有用金漆写有一对窄条楹联曰"万福攸同财恒足，源兴共乐利自生"，这副联用正楷书写，字体虽小但用笔浑厚有力，作为宾客到访迎面的"口号"自然是屋主十分在意的，可以依此从侧面了解全屋的中国传统吉祥纹饰的核心思想。另有一类是牌匾，它是中国传统建筑中较有功能性的文字装饰，它往往出现于门厅隔断的正上方，在我国江南一带的古建庭院中也经常出现在屏门的正上方，娘惹建筑中的屏门与牌匾的组合较少，如"鼎门甲第"匾。而进屏门虽无与之有直接组合接触的牌匾，但是其正对面的"燕翼贻谋"匾与其置于同一空间中，其重视子孙后代发展的含义同样也可以用于补充解释进屏门上装饰所传达的精神追求。值得一提的是，在马六甲峇峇娘惹祖屋博物馆（Baba and Nyonya Heritage Museum）中的屏门左右小门横批上就镶有写满"九叠篆"的构件（图7），译为"一团和气，福满华堂"。

图7 "九叠篆"的木雕构件　　　　　　　　　　　　图8 "广东太平门外源昌街赵三友造"款

四、娘惹建筑中屏门的装饰工艺

　　关于娘惹建筑中屏门装饰的工艺，我们不妨从它的作坊着手了解。娘惹博物馆原名"海记栈"，是清末广东增城（今属广州市）著名华侨郑景贵[1]在槟城的私宅，进屏门的槅心木雕上虽有"义和造"款，现已无从考据，但同一建筑中的其他木雕装饰留有关键信息。在进屏门的背面正对一面雕刻繁复华丽的飞罩，在其左下角落有款曰"广东太平门外源昌街赵三友造"（图8）。单从艺术风格和雕刻手法上看，该飞罩与进屏门上的装饰工艺相近。综上，我们结合中国传统古建木雕工艺并侧重广派木雕，足以窥探一二。

　　广派木雕历史悠久，以潮州、广州、佛山三地的木雕为代表，而潮州木雕因其精湛的雕工，名声最盛。清代中叶至民国中期是广派木雕最为兴盛的时期，木雕技艺远播海外。据考证，"赵三友"应是清光绪年间广派著名木雕字号"三友堂"的一个支系[2]，时间上涵盖了槟城的娘惹博物馆落成的时间（1895年，即清光绪二十一年），而"太平门外源昌街"今地具体所在已不可考，但通过相关资料可知，太平门今在广州市人民南路沙面附近，所以该作坊门店或与广州十三行有关。广派木雕的雕刻技法包含沉雕、薄雕、浮雕、通雕等多种，而其中以通雕最为卓越，通过多平面雕刻，物象层层叠叠，交错穿插，使作品具有强烈的艺术感染力[3]。进屏门中门扇的槅心处以及侧门花飞罩的主体纹饰即运用高浮雕结合通雕的手

[1] 广州市地方志编纂委员会编：《广州市志》卷十九《人物志》，广州出版社，1996年，第374页。
[2] 王海娜：《试论佛山木雕及其保护》，《广州文博·4》，文物出版社，2011年。
[3] 吴丽娥：《清光绪大神龛的装饰艺术》，《中国文物报》2023年2月21日第4版。

法，在平面视觉的感受中展现各个物象的空间关系，从不同的角度观赏，通透立体，栩栩如生。此外，进屏门还运用正面贴雕（高浮雕）和背面浅刻相结合的方式，将同一个样式的门扇裙板或者绦环板，"一凸一凹""阴阳向背"形成强烈的视觉对比和节奏关系，富有变化，例如裙板的"梅花"与"牡丹"，上束腰绦环板的"瓜蝶"与"秋葵"。

上彩是雕刻后的工艺步骤，娘惹建筑中的木雕构件主要以"暗红地""金漆纹"的色彩搭配，艺术风格与闽南、潮州一带的金漆木雕相一致。其中以贴金工艺最具特色，贴金工艺主要包含打磨胎体、髹漆、贴金或描金等步骤，过程中需要对漆料的配比、漆面的平整度、干湿把握程度都要有丰富的实践经验。有了漆面的保护，在鲜活雕刻艺术的同时，也免受沿海气候环境对木质构件的破坏。

在艺术性方面，屏门装饰的吉祥纹样有良好的传统和完善的工序，工匠们会依照粉本在雕刻之初在木料上描绘样稿，按绘画构图的逻辑来理解，样稿线图与木雕的关系就是白描艺术与雕刻艺术相互转换，而在这其中特别是以浮雕、通雕为主的艺术语言，就是将中国绘画艺术中的平面造型意蕴转换为一种空间立体关系的过程。在设计构成方面，进屏门木雕构件最直接的布局形式是对称，它是"成双"含义在雕刻工匠中的美学实践，从整体上看，进屏门的构件量为偶数，左右空间相对应的纹饰是一致的。从局部看，例如侧门花飞罩因其构成的特性，也是对称的，而且在把握左右对称美感的基础上又做了变化，使整体视觉不失衡又耐看。这种在形式上的布局强调，无疑为装饰的内容叠加深刻的文化含义，其中还包括中国传统美学强烈的秩序意识。另外，我们对娘惹建筑中的木雕第一感观往往是构图密集饱满，富有细节，这符合潮州木雕周身布饰的艺术风格和视觉效果。而在潮州的木雕艺术中，这种构成现象被称为"装堂花"形式[1]。

五、意义与评价

通过上述分析，透过"屏门"这一视角以小见大，无论是"福""禄""寿"主题纹饰还是在此文化体系下的动植物纹饰，都是中国传统建筑文化的重要组成部分，它们承载着人们对美好生活的精神寄托。娘惹建筑深刻把握这一精神内涵，在高度认同华人文化根源的同时，注重自身在海外安身立命，兴旺壮大的境况，同时包含了对后代子女即"峇峇娘惹"的教育与期盼。受此影响，家庭居住的环境就显得尤为重要，这里作为他们的生活起居的场所，更是他们人生的第一课堂，因此，纹饰不仅有蕴含"福禄寿喜""成双成对""财运亨通""广结善缘""添丁添福"等对幸福、财富、成功和长寿的美好祝愿和追求，更体现了激励后辈积极向上生活的精神与态度。通过在以"屏门"为典型的建筑木构件上使用这些吉祥纹饰，中国传统文化得以传承和延续。它们成为了历史文化的载体，让后代能够了解和感受先辈们的价值观和审美观念，促进文化的传承和发展。同时，这些纹饰也体现了峇峇娘惹对中国传统文化中的家庭、社会和人生等价值观的认同，是中华文化在海外传播的见证，具有深刻的文化交流内涵和历史性的意义。

---

[1] 卓莎：《花鸟题材潮州木雕构图渊源考释》，《大众文艺》2021年第23期。

新加坡土生文化馆：
展示东南亚土生社群的跨文化艺术

新加坡土生文化馆

一、谁是土生群体？

东南亚的土生群体是多元遗产交融的社群，源自沿着贯穿中国、南亚、中东和欧洲的海上贸易路线往来的商贾和行旅。一些商旅在途经东南亚港口时选择定居，与当地人通婚，由此逐渐形成了独特的土生社群。

"土生"，即Peranakan一词来源于马来语词根"anak"，意思是"孩子"，含有"本地出生"的意思。以"土生"自称的社群包括土生华人（亦称海峡华人或峇峇娘惹）、土生印度人（或称马六甲仄迪人）、土生爪哇人、土生阿拉伯人等多个不同社群，以及其他类似的土生群体。

土生社群的共同特征在于文化的融合：将东南亚之外的祖先文化（中国、印度、阿拉伯、欧洲）融入马来群岛的本土文化。这种交融催生了丰富多彩的多元混合文化。

土生华人主要是中国南方商人的后裔，他们的文化融合了中国和东南亚的传统，也受到欧洲的影响。土生华人社群的形成可追溯至16世纪早期的印尼和马来半岛[1]。到19世纪，这些社群已经在槟城（图1）、马六甲、新加坡和巴达维亚（今雅加达）（图2）等地扎根，并进一步向北延伸至缅甸仰光和泰国普吉岛[2]。如今，土生华人社群遍布马来西亚、新加坡、印度尼西亚和文莱，也见于曼谷、普吉岛、仰光，甚至远至澳大利亚。

马六甲仄迪人（或称土生印度人）的祖先主要是15世纪早期移居马六甲的南印度印度教泰米尔商人。他们与当地的马来人、爪哇人、巴塔克人，以及马六甲的峇峇娘惹通婚[3]。到20世纪初，一部分土生印度

[1] Joo Ee Khoo. 1996. The Straits Chinese: A Cultural History. Amsterdam: Pepin Press. p. 18.

[2] Peter Lee. 2014. Sarong Kebaya: Peranakan Fashion in an Interconnected World 1500-1950. Singapore: Asian Civilisations Museum. pp. 95.

[3] Samuel S Dhoraisingam. 2005. Peranakan Indians of Singapore and Melaka: Indian Babas and Nyonyas – Chitty Melaka. Singapore: Institute of Southeast Asian Studies. pp. 4.

图1 叶福兴（Yeap Hock Hin）夫妇结婚照
1930年左右
明胶银盐印相
土生文化馆 藏
Lee Kip Lee夫妇 赠

图2 Lie Pa-toe Nio 肖像
爪哇巴达维亚（雅加达），1990年左右
明胶银盐印相（手工着色）
土生文化馆 藏

图3 阿鲁穆甘·苏普拉马尼亚姆·厌迪
（Arumugam Supramaniam Chitty）
和西瓦伽米（Sivagamee）肖像照
新加坡，20世纪30年代
明胶银盐印相
土生文化馆 藏
Ponnosamy Kalastree先生 赠

人迁居至槟城、吉隆坡和新加坡，并在该地区建立了自己的社群[1]（图3）。

　　土生爪哇人是印度次人陆穆斯林商人的后裔，其祖辈与东南亚的马来族及其他土著女性通婚。在马来西亚，这些社群至今仍坚持其"伊斯兰教价值观和身份认同"[2]，主要集中在槟城、吉打、马六甲和霹雳[3]，但在新加坡及东南亚其他地区也有分布（图4）。

[1] Samuel S Dhoraisingam. 2005. Peranakan Indians of Singapore and Melaka: Indian Babas and Nyonyas – Chitty Melaka. Singapore: Institute of Southeast Asian Studies. pp. 18.

[2] Wazir Jahan Karim. 2020. Feasts of Penang: Muslim Culinary Heritage. Malaysia: MPH Group Publishing Sdn Bhd. pp. 21.

[3] Omar Yusoff. 2010. Sejarah pembentukan Jawi Peranakan Pulau Pinang. In: O. Yusoff & J. Aziz. Jawi Peranakan di Pulau Pinang: Ekspresi sebuah identity. Malaysia: Penerbit Universiti Sains Malaysia. pp. 4.

图4 直落古楼的土生爪哇人家庭
新加坡，1932年11月23日
明胶银盐印相
由艾哈迈德·默罕默德·易卜拉欣
（Ahmad Mohamed Ibrahim）的家族
借展至土生文化馆

图5 莎丽法·阿威雅·阿裕（Sharifah
Alwiyah Aljunied）和她的女儿们
新加坡，20世纪50年代
明胶银盐印相
由已故赛义德·侯赛因·哈龙·阿裕尼先生
（Syed Hussain bin Haroon Aljunied）的家族
借展至土生文化馆

　　土生阿拉伯人是穆斯林商人的后裔，其祖先定居于东南亚，与当地社群通婚，同时仍然深刻认同阿拉伯传统。东南亚的许多土生阿拉伯人可溯源至也门的哈德拉毛。除从事贸易活动外，阿拉伯商人前往东南亚的另一个重要动机是传播伊斯兰教[1]（图5）。

　　所有土生社群的发展都深受欧洲殖民的影响。从葡萄牙到荷兰，再到英国，殖民者统治了许多土生社群居住的东南亚港口城市。他们统治下的贸易网络不仅推动了商品流通[2]，也促进了服饰、饮食、语言等文化形式的传播[3]。

[1] Pue Giok Hun. 2016. Peranakan as Plural Identity: Cases from Peninsular Malaysia. Regional Journal of Southeast Asian Studies, (1)1: 79.

[2] Joo Ee Khoo. 1996. The Straits Chinese: A Cultural History. Amsterdam: Pepin Press. pp.18-20.

[3] Peter Lee. 2014. Sarong Kebaya: Peranakan Fashion in an Interconnected World 1500-1950. Singapore: Asian Civilisations Museum. pp. 120-124.

图6　新加坡土生文化馆
土生文化馆供图

二、土生文化馆的历史

土生文化馆展示了东南亚土生社群的艺术与文化，是东南亚土生文物领域内最精美、最全面的公立收藏机构之一。文化馆隶属于新加坡国家文物局下的亚洲文明博物馆（图6）。

土生文化馆的收藏最初来源于亚洲文明博物馆的东南亚收藏。这部分藏品最早属于19世纪的莱佛士图书馆和博物馆，之后划归新加坡国家博物馆。1993年，新加坡国家博物馆将该部分藏品划拨至亚洲文明博物馆[1]。

---

[1] Ibrahim Tahir, Valerie Ho. (eds.) 2017. Peranakan Museum Guide. Singapore: Asian Civilisations Museum for the Peranakan Museum. p. 15.

自20世纪80年代起，新加坡国家博物馆便着手为其常设展厅积极收藏土生文物。1993年，亚洲文明博物馆成立之后，公众和社区对土生文化的兴趣日益浓厚，将其视为"真正的新加坡文化的典范"。这一趋势促使博物馆的土生文物收藏大幅增长，最终于2008年4月开设了专门的土生文化馆[1]。

经过十年的运营，土生文化馆于2019年闭馆，开展了为期四年的翻新工程。2023年2月17日，土生文化馆以焕然一新的展厅重新面向公众开放。土生文化馆坐落在一座新古典主义风格的建筑内，该建筑始建于1910至1912年，最早曾是道南学校所在地[2]。

三、展厅

土生文化馆共有三层展厅，分别以"起源""家""风格"为主题，从身份认同的角度探索土生世界。展厅采用交错式陈列方式，使得反映土生物质文化的实物与凸显非物质文化遗产多样性的社区访谈、照片、视频交相呼应。这些非物质文化遗产包括针线和刺绣技艺、语言、饮食文化、节庆习俗、宗教仪式，以及与服饰和发型相关的生活传统等。展览的最后，各展厅还呈现了土生文化的当代表达形式，包括当代艺术、时尚、设计和手工艺品，为观众提供丰富多彩的参观体验。

文化馆并未提供"土生"一词的单一定义，而是从这样的视角出发，探索何谓土生身份：它是一种发生在马来—印尼地区，并更广泛地存在于东南亚的文化现象，外来的商人和行旅来这里定居、通婚，并逐渐适应了当地的风俗和传统。由于身份标志依赖于具体的地方环境，并可能随着时间推移而发生变化，因此，是否自我认同为"土生"便成了定义身份的一个关键因素。此外，不同个体的选择和群体观点的差异，也意味着"土生"身份可以有多种定义。

一楼的"起源"展厅向观众介绍了多元化的土生社群（图7）。展厅中陈列着来自马来-印尼地区的文物，展示了他们称之为"家"的物质文化；同时，还配有一个互动地图，直观地呈现他们的起源地分布。观众可以通过互动语言功能聆听东南亚港口城市多语言环境中的对话，特别是融合了福建话和马来语的土生语言——峇峇马来话（Baba Malay）。这些陈列和互动都辅有照片和视频访谈，启发观众思考"是什么造就了土生身份或特质？"（图8）。"起源"展厅的另一重要特色在于合作开发过程。土生文化馆与新加坡的土生社区协会，以及一些热心人士密切商议合作，共同打造了这一展厅，这些人士慷慨地贡献了关于语言的专业知识、照片，以及访谈，丰富了展厅内容。

二楼的四个展厅以"家"为主题，通过文物陈列呈现不同的文化影响如何交汇，催生出独特的物质文化，以及土生传统、饮食习俗、语言和宗教信仰等一系列非物质文化。其中三个展厅展示了家具（图9）、肖像、照片、银器（图10），以及文学和音乐（图11），勾勒出土生家庭和社区生活面貌；另有仪式相关物件，呈现了土生社群的宗教活动（图12）。第四间展厅重点展示土生家庭使用的陶瓷和炊具（图13），

[1] Ibrahim Tahir, Valerie Ho. (eds.) 2017. Peranakan Museum Guide. Singapore: Asian Civilisations Museum for the Peranakan Museum. pp.17-18.

[2] Ibrahim Tahir, Valerie Ho. (eds.) 2017. Peranakan Museum Guide. Singapore: Asian Civilisations Museum for the Peranakan Museum. p. 15.

图7 "起源"展厅中的马来群岛文物陈列
　　　土生文化馆供图

图8 "起源"展厅中的照片陈列
　　　土生文化馆供图

图10 圣杯
可能产自中国，1905年
银
土生文化馆 藏
Ong Poh Neo 赠

图9 供桌边柜
新加坡，1900—1920年
柚木
土生文化馆 藏
T.W.Ong家族 赠

图11 收音留声机
英国或新加坡，20世纪中期
木，金属线，塑料，电子元件
土生文化馆 藏

图12 桌帏
印度尼西亚，20世纪早期
棉（彩绘峇迪）
土生文化馆 藏
Matthew 与 Alice Yapp 赠

图13 带有赛义德·阿卜杜勒·拉赫曼·塔哈·阿沙戈夫
（Syed Abdul Rahman bin Taha Alsagoff，Engku
Aman，1880-1955）字母缩写的茶壶
英国J.& G. Meakin公司，20世纪
瓷器
由Arab Network @ Singapore机构代表
赛义德·阿卜杜勒·拉赫曼·塔哈·阿沙戈夫家族
借展至土生文化馆

其中包括本地称为"娘惹瓷器（nyonyaware）"的多彩釉上彩瓷器（图14）。最后，展厅中还有社区成员参与的一系列视频，探索了土生饮食文化这一重要且延续至今的传统。土生饮食融合了中国、南亚、中东和东南亚的烹饪风味，同时也深受欧洲影响。

三楼展厅展示了土生"风格"，展品包括峇迪[1]（图15）、装饰织物（图16）、珠宝（图17、图18）、时装与配饰。陈列的文物表明，数百年来，土生文化的审美一直受到东南亚港口城市的多元文化影响，许多形式、图案与元素在发展过程中吸收、借鉴并融合了本地其他社群的传统。最后一个展厅以"纱笼可峇雅"作为展览的尾声（图19）。纱笼可峇雅是一种独特而优雅的服装，已经成为土生身份的象征。然而，长期以来，这类服装也广泛流行于海洋东南亚的多个社群，并且各个社区也发展出了自己独特的风格。

[1] batik，一种蜡染印花布，或用蜡染布制作的衣服。

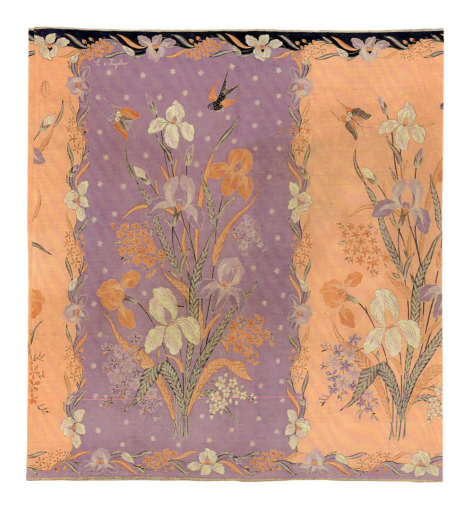

图15 纱笼
爪哇，北加浪岸，约1940年
棉质（彩绘峇迪）
土生文化馆 藏
Eliza van Zuylen 赠

图16 桌布
槟城，约1920年
棉质针绣底布，欧洲玻璃种珠
土生文化馆 藏
由法国巴黎银行基金会和法国巴黎银行
新加坡分行赞助修复

图17 带扣腰带
新加坡或海峡殖民地，20世纪早期
黄金，钻石
土生文化馆 藏
Edmond Chin先生 赠

图18 项链
新加坡，20世纪早期
银镀金
土生文化馆 藏
Knight Glenn Jeyasingam夫人 赠

图19　土生文化馆的时装展厅
土生文化馆 供图

　　东南亚的土生社群一向展现出高度的适应力，能够灵活吸纳不同文化，并自然地融入当地环境。展厅中的展品凝聚了中国、东南亚、南亚以及欧洲文化的影响，生动呈现了土生生活中多元文化交织的丰富内涵。

后记

  本书是中国（海南）南海博物馆在2024年3月至7月期间举办的"峇峇娘惹的世界——海上丝绸之路上的峇峇娘惹文化展"配套图录。该展览由中国（海南）南海博物馆策划，展出来自新加坡亚洲文明博物馆和新加坡土生文化馆藏品。

  付梓之际，再次感谢中国文物保护基金会在展览资金上的大力支持；感谢新加坡亚洲文明博物馆、新加坡土生文化馆和新加坡文物保护中心在文物借展等方面提供的帮助；还要感谢中国科技出版传媒股份有限公司在图书编辑出版中付出的辛勤劳动。

  展览图录是展览内容的延伸，并以纸本化的形式保留下来。本书除了传递展览方面的内容，还为读者在多元文化融合、峇峇娘惹文化、海上丝绸之路研究等方面提供资料借鉴。由于编者专业水平有限，书中难免有疏漏之处，尚请专家、学者批评指正。

编者

2024 年 11 月

Afterword

This book is the companion volume to the exhibition "Exploring the World of Baba Nyonya: A Peranakan Culture Exhibition on the Maritime Silk Road" held at the China (Hainan) Museum of the South China Sea from March to July 2024. The exhibition is curated by the China (Hainan) Museum of the South China Sea featuring loans from the collections of the Asian Civilisations Museum and the Peranakan Museum.

As we go to press, we would like to express our gratitude once again to the China Foundation for Cultural Heritage Conservation for their generous financial support of the exhibition. We are also thankful to the Asian Civilisations Museum, the Peranakan Museum, and the Heritage Conservation Centre in Singapore for their assistance with the loan of artefacts. Our appreciation also extends to China Science Publishing & Media Ltd. for their diligent efforts in editing and publishing this book.

This exhibition catalogue serves as an extension of the exhibition content, preserving it in print form. Beyond conveying the exhibition material, it offers readers valuable references for research on multicultural integration, Baba Nyonya culture, and the Maritime Silk Road. Despite our best efforts, we acknowledge that there may be omissions or inaccuracies due to the editors' limited expertise. We sincerely welcome constructive criticism and corrections from experts and scholars in the field.

The Editors
November 2024